STRAIGHT
TALK *about*
GOSPEL
PRINCIPLES

STRAIGHT TALK *about* GOSPEL PRINCIPLES

ALLAN K. BURGESS
MAX H. MOLGARD

BOOKCRAFT
Salt Lake City, Utah

Library of Congress Catalog Card Number: 94-78426
ISBN 0-88494-953-2

First Printing, 1994

Printed in the United States of America

Contents

Introduction

When Korihor, the antichrist, ridiculed Alma concerning the existence of a God, Alma asked Korihor a very important question: "And now what evidence have ye that there is no God, or that Christ cometh not? I say unto you that ye have none, save it be your word only." (Alma 30:40.)

Alma then went on to explain all of the evidences that he had of God's reality. By doing so, Alma turned the tables on Korihor. Korihor had wanted Alma to prove that there was a God. Before Alma stated his proof, however, he first asked Korihor to supply evidence that there was no God. Korihor, of course, had no such evidence, and Alma's bold tactic exposed the fallacy of Korihor's claim.

When we examine a topic, we usually take the approach of finding out what it is or what it does. This, however, only gives us a partial view or understanding. We can often come to a clearer understanding by looking at something from a different point of view. Rather than just trying to prove God's existence, Alma took a different approach by asking Korihor to prove there was no God. Similarly, the approach we take in this book is to examine various principles and practices of the gospel not only for what they are and do but also for what they are not and don't do. Many times as we see what something is not, we develop a better understanding of what it is.

A good example of this occurred when Satan appeared to Moses after Moses had seen God and all of his glory. Satan demanded that Moses worship him. Moses' reply to Satan clearly demonstrates that Moses knew who Satan was and who he was not. But more important, by knowing this he also clearly understood who God was and what his relationship to him was:

> And it came to pass that Moses looked upon Satan and said: Who art thou? For behold, I am a son of God, in the similitude of his Only Begotten; and where is thy glory, that I should worship thee?
>
> For behold, I could not look upon God, except his glory should come upon me, and I were transfigured before him. But I can look upon thee in the natural man. Is it not so, surely?
>
> Blessed be the name of my God, for his Spirit hath not altogether withdrawn from me, or else where is thy glory, for it is darkness unto me? And I can judge between thee and God; for God said unto me; Worship God, for him only shalt thou serve. (Moses 1:13–15.)

Both Alma and Moses spoke plainly to their adversaries in order to clarify what was and wasn't correct. Our intent is likewise to talk straight about various principles and practices of the gospel. By doing so, we hope the reader will come away with a better understanding of the topics covered and develop a greater commitment to follow the Savior and his teachings.

1

The Purpose of Life

A few years ago, several leaders were asked to plan a meeting for 120 seminary teachers. When they asked what the purpose of the meeting was, they drew blank stares. No one had decided on a purpose—they had simply felt that there should be a meeting. The leaders decided that they could do little effective planning until they knew the purpose for the meeting.

Recently a middle-aged couple went to the temple with their children, where they were sealed as an eternal family. For several months before this important event, however, the father had been embezzling funds from his employer. He had lied to his bishop and stake president about his honesty and had knelt across the altar as though he were worthy to be there. It is difficult to imagine the man's purposes for going to the temple. Obviously he had no idea of the importance of the covenants he was making and the role that obedience plays in making family ties eternal.

It is difficult for us to be successful in any important endeavor until we know what the purpose of that endeavor is. So it is with our lives here on earth. Until we know why we are here and what we came here to accomplish, it is almost impossible to successfully fulfill our purpose here. When we understand the purpose of this earth life, we also better understand other things, such as the purpose of the commandments, our meetings, and the Lord's church.

What the Purpose of Life Is Not

The purpose of life is not just to get a body or be tested. Many Church members do not fully understand the main purpose for our being here on earth. When asked the purpose of life, they give such answers as: "We are here to be tested." "We are here to get a body." "We are here to keep the commandments." These answers are not wrong as much as incomplete. They are like looking at a picture of a yard comprised of a home, trees, flowers, lawn, and a basketball court and saying that the picture is of only a basketball court or a tree. The picture is of a yard, and identifying it as anything less is not only inaccurate but also confusing.

One danger in not seeing the complete picture of why we are here is that we might focus on one area—such as getting a body or being tested—and fail to accomplish what we came here to do. Getting a body, keeping the commandments, and being tested are only means to an end, not the end itself. As we begin to focus on the final goal instead of the intermediary steps, we find ourselves approaching life differently. How we approach our meetings, serve in the Church, view the commandments, treat others, and feel about life will all begin to change.

What the Purpose of Life Is

1. The purpose of life is to become like God—to become gods ourselves. Jesus invited us to take this divine journey when he said, "What manner of men ought ye to be? Verily I say unto you, even as I am." (3 Nephi 27:27.) The Prophet Joseph Smith declared, "If you wish to go where God is, you must be like God, or possess the principles which God possesses" (*Teachings of the Prophet Joseph Smith*, p. 216).

We did not come here just to do but rather to become. Our purpose is not merely to do honest things but to become honest; not just to do charitable acts but to become charitable. If our hearts are right and our motives pure, doing will lead to becoming. The prophet Mormon referred to this significant truth when he said, "Pray unto the Father with all the energy of heart, that ye may be filled with this love, which he hath bestowed upon all who are true followers of his Son, Jesus Christ; . . . that when he shall appear we shall be like him" (Moroni 7:48). Notice the emphasis on becoming charitable rather than on doing charitable things.

If we are not careful, we may fall into the trap of ritual obedience. We may go to church because it is the right thing to do rather than because we want to worship, learn, and make covenants with our Father in Heaven. We may do our home teaching or visiting teaching because our ward is striving for 100 percent teaching or because we have forty-three straight months without a miss or because our companion bugs us to go. Such motivation often does little to help us become more like God. As we ponder the real purpose of home or visiting teaching and then begin to visit the families out of concern for their welfare, our love for them will deepen and our nature will become more Godlike. This same principle applies to every commandment that God has given us.

We are not suggesting that we will become completely like God during this lifetime, but we can begin this journey and become much more like him than we are now. Elder Neal A. Maxwell explained: "As we accept Christ and become his children, there begins to be a change—even a 'mighty change' in us. As we earnestly strive to become one with him and his purposes, *we come to resemble him.* Christ who has saved us thus becomes the Father of our Salvation, and we become the 'children of Christ,' having his image increasing in our countenance and conduct (see Mosiah 5:7)." (*BYU 1998–90 Devotional and Fireside Speeches,* p. 87.)

Notice that we begin to resemble Christ when we strive to become one with his purposes. It takes more than rote obedience to change our basic nature and attitudes. We must understand what God's purposes are and desire to fulfill them.

This mighty change does not and, even more important, cannot be performed alone. It is not solely a matter of willpower and self-control. President Ezra Taft Benson has promised us that God will come to our aid and help us obtain the power to change our lives. Along with this promise, he gave the following important warning:

We must be careful, as we seek to become more and more godlike, that we do not become discouraged and lose hope. Becoming Christlike is a lifetime pursuit and very often involves growth and change that is slow, almost imperceptible. The scriptures record remarkable accounts of men whose lives changed dramatically, in an instant, as it were. . . .

But we must be cautious as we discuss these remarkable examples. Though they are real and powerful, they are the exception more than the rule. For every Paul, for every Enos, and for every King Lamoni, there are hundreds and thousands of people who find the process of repentance much more subtle, much more imperceptible. Day by day they move closer to the Lord, little realizing they are building a godlike life. They live quiet lives of goodness, service, and commitment. . . .

. . . The Lord is pleased with every effort, even the tiny, daily ones in which we strive to be more like Him. (*Ensign,* October 1989, p. 5.)

As the intentions and desires of our hearts change and we begin to develop the attributes of God, we increase our access to God's power. This growth does not spring from superficial obedience but is the companion of a sincere desire to serve God. It comes when we obey God because we love him and want to please him. It comes when we place him first in our lives. It comes when we remember why we are here and why God wants us to keep the commandments. Elder Maxwell put it this way:

Real righteousness, therefore, cannot be a superficial, ritualistic thing. It must arise out of the deepest convictions of the soul, not out of a desire merely to "go along" with the Heavenly Regime simply because that's how things are done! God's power—unlike mortal power—is accessed only by those who have developed, to a requisite degree, God's attributes. (*Ensign,* July 1982, p. 53.)

Elder Richard G. Scott summed up what we have been discussing when he stated, "Righteous character is what you *are*. It is more important than what you own, what you have learned, or what you have accomplished." (*Ensign,* May 1989, p. 37.)

2. Another purpose for life is to gain a fulness of joy. The prophet Lehi taught that "Adam fell that men might be; and men are, that they might have joy" (2 Nephi 2:25). As we lived with our Father in Heaven in our pre-earthly existence, we saw how happy he was. This must have influenced our decision to come here so we could become like him and enjoy that same happiness. Since we are going to be discussing the subject of happiness in another chapter, we will limit our discussion here; however, it is important to realize that God has created a world that offers everything we need to become like him and receive a fulness of joy.

2

Sin

What Sin Is Not

1. **S**in is not freedom. Satan is the author of sin. His sole objective is to get us to give up our freedom and serve him. The more control he has over us, the more power he has. He is bent on gaining all the power he can and will do whatever he can to get it. Heavenly Father's goal is just the opposite. He wants us to be free and knows the only way we can truly become so is by living free of sin. Amulek explained:

> Ye cannot say, when ye are brought to that awful crisis, that I will repent, that I will return to my God. Nay, ye cannot say this; for that same spirit which doth possess your bodies at the time that ye go out of this life, that same spirit will have power to possess your body in that eternal world.
>
> For behold, if ye have procrastinated the day of your repentance even until death, behold, ye have become subjected to the spirit of the devil, and he doth seal you his; therefore, the Spirit of the Lord hath withdrawn from you, and hath no place in you, and the devil hath all power over you; and this is the final state of the wicked. (Alma 34:34–35.)

In his efforts to deprive us of our freedom, Satan throws a barrage of temptations at us. Many of the temptations appeal to our bodily desires. As we give in to these temptations, Satan not only takes control of our bodies but also strives to put our spirits in bondage.

Disobeying the Word of Wisdom exemplifies this principle. Elder Hartman Rector, Jr., once told of a Church member who returned to his former habit of smoking cigarettes. The man excused his smoking by saying that he didn't want to smoke but felt that he couldn't help it. In effect he was saying that he had let his body rule over his spirit; he had allowed his body to become boss.

The man finally suffered a stroke. His whole body was paralyzed—except his right arm and his eyes—when his son-in-law found him on the porch of his house. As the son-in-law picked him up, the man reached for the cigarette in his son-in-law's mouth. Because he could not hold onto it, his son-in-law held the lighted cigarette to the stricken man's numb lips. He could neither hold the cigarette in his mouth nor smoke it properly, but his body still cried for its nicotine fix.

The man spent the next nine months lying in bed. He wore out the pocket of his pajamas reaching into it for a cigarette that was not there. Eventually the man died and went to the spirit world. Elder Rector then asked an important question: "Do you suppose he still wants a cigarette? On the basis of Amulek's statement, he does. But there is just one catch—there are no cigarettes in the spirit world. Would you suppose he is in paradise or in spirit prison? The answer seems only too obvious." (See Conference Report, October 1970, p. 74.)

It becomes a clear choice. We can either choose to have as our master Jesus Christ, who makes us free, or Satan, who imprisons our souls. Jesus explained it this way: "Whosoever committeth sin is the servant of sin" (John 8:34).

President N. Eldon Tanner taught: "There is no happiness in sin, and when we depart from the path of righteousness we begin to do those things which will inevitably lead us to unhappiness and misery and loss of freedom" (*Ensign,* May 1977, p. 17).

2. Sin is never right. Satan would have us believe that under certain circumstances it is all right to commit a little sin. After all, we *can* repent. Nephi warned us of this attitude that Satan would promote in our day:

Yea, and there shall be many which shall say: Eat, drink, and be merry, for tomorrow we die; and it shall be well with us.

And there shall also be many which shall say: Eat, drink, and be merry; nevertheless, fear God—he will justify in committing a little sin; yea, lie a little, take the advantage of one because of his words, dig a pit for thy neighbor; there is no harm in this; and do all these things, for tomorrow we die; and if it so be that we are guilty, God will beat us with a few stripes, and at last we shall be saved in the kingdom of God. (2 Nephi 28:7–8.)

The Lord made it clear where he stands when he said: "For I the Lord cannot look upon sin with the least degree of allowance" (D&C 1:31). The Lord has great love and mercy and will forgive us as we repent; but sin is sin, and he can never say it is otherwise. He knows that no matter what our excuse for sinning may be, the consequences must always be the same: we will lose the Spirit and eventually eternal life with God.

3. Sin will never save us. In Amulek's debate with Zeezrom, the antichrist, he stated:

And I say unto you again that he cannot save them in their sins; for I cannot deny his word, and he hath said that no unclean thing can inherit the kingdom of heaven; therefore, how can ye be saved, except ye inherit the kingdom of heaven? Therefore, ye cannot be saved in your sins. (Alma 11:37.)

Real happiness can only come as we live righteously. None of us are perfect, but as we strive to live a life void of sin and full of goodness, we can experience real happiness. A fulness of joy can only be experienced by gaining eternal life, which is life with God. If we are to have life with him we must be like him—without sin. We should always remember what Paul taught the Romans: "For the wages of sin is death; but the gift of God is eternal life through Jesus Christ our Lord" (Romans 6:23).

What Sin Is

1. Sin saps spiritual power from our lives. Elder Angel Abrea related the following story:

> One extremely hot afternoon I was crossing the green agricultural lands of the Pampas in Argentina. The sun was scorching the highway to the point that the heat waves became visible. Nevertheless, I was confident and comfortable because I had just purchased a brand-new car, fresh from the factory, with a big motor and plenty of power to conquer the elements and allow me to travel briskly in air-conditioned comfort.
>
> Suddenly, I noticed that the temperature in my new car had begun to climb and the big motor began to show signs of strain. When the temperature gauge got to the danger point, I pulled the car over to the side of the road in the hope that with my very limited knowledge of mechanics I could discover what was wrong with the car. I must admit I was rather disgusted to think that something could stop my big new car. It wasn't long after I had lifted the hood that I discovered, to my amazement, that a myriad of colorful little butterflies had collected on the radiator, choked off the cooling process, and stopped the car. (*Ensign*, November 1981, p. 23.)

Our life is very much like Elder Abrea's car. We have been given, through the gospel of Jesus Christ, the power and potential to become like our Heavenly Father. Nothing can stop us from reaching that potential except sin. Sin in our lives can be just as disabling to us as the butterflies were to the car. Each little butterfly that collected on the radiator of the car took more and more power from the engine, until finally it could no longer operate properly. Likewise, sin unrepented of in our lives can disable us until we can no longer operate properly.

2. Sin is the thief of all that is good in our lives, now and throughout eternity. Jeremiah simply stated, "Your sins have withholden good things from you" (Jeremiah 5:25). If we are to have the great blessings the Lord has in store for us, we must watch for the thief of sin in our lives. We can never put down our guard, for in the

moment we do, sin will try to overtake us and steal from us the blessings that could be ours.

3. Sin is overcome through obedience to right teachings and through the power of God. Only by humble obedience to God's commandments can we combat sin and eventually defeat it. A good example of this is the experience of a young man who joined the Church. The man and his wife were both users of tobacco, and, after being taught about the Word of Wisdom by the missionaries, they decided, "Well, if that is what the Lord wants and if this is the Lord's church, we will try it."

The man was not particularly concerned about himself. He thought he could quit smoking easily. But he was concerned about his wife; she had never tried to quit before. On the other hand, he had quit several times. Quitting hadn't been too difficult before, although staying off the cigarettes permanently had presented problems. This time, to his surprise, his wife quit without any apparent problems, but he had tremendous difficulty. He became nervous and irritable. He was cranky at work and could not sleep at night. One night he became so restless and disturbed that his wife suggested that he pray and ask Heavenly Father for help. He ridiculed the idea of prayer and said: "This is something I have to do. Nobody can help me with this. I can do this." But as the night passed and he tried in vain everything he could to get to sleep, he finally humbled himself enough to kneel at the side of the bed and prayed vocally.

According to his own testimony, he got up from his prayer, got into bed, went to sleep, and has never been tempted by cigarettes since. (See Eldred G. Smith, Conference Report, April 1955, p. 42.)

We can learn an important principle from this man's experience. When we try to make major changes on our own, Satan is standing by to help us with discouragement and failure. But when we are willing to humbly put ourselves in God's hands, we can expect his divine help. Miracles can and do happen when we put our faith in him.

3

Repentance

What Repentance Is Not

1. Repentance is not just stopping something wrong or starting something right. True repentance involves faith, the Savior, and a "mighty change of heart." President Ezra Taft Benson explained this when he wrote:

> Many men and women in the world demonstrate great willpower and self-discipline in overcoming bad habits and the weaknesses of the flesh. Yet at the same time they give no thought to the Master, sometimes even openly rejecting Him. Such changes of behavior, even if in a positive direction, do not constitute true repentance.
>
> Faith in the Lord Jesus Christ is the foundation upon which sincere and meaningful repentance must be built. (*Ensign*, October 1989, p. 2.)

2. Repentance is not simply suffering or sorrowing for sin. Sometimes people feel they are repentant because their sins have brought suffering into their lives. They may even feel some sorrow for

their sins, but this is not repentance either. Elder Theodore M. Burton clarified these misconceptions when he explained:

> Many times a bishop will write, "I feel he has suffered enough!" But suffering is not repentance. Suffering comes from *lack* of complete repentance. A stake president will write, "I feel he has been punished enough!" But punishment is not repentance. Punishment *follows* disobedience and *precedes* repentance. A husband will write, "My wife has confessed everything!" But confession is not repentance. Confession is an admission of guilt that occurs as repentance begins. A wife will write, "My husband is filled with remorse!" But remorse is not repentance. Remorse and sorrow continue because a person has *not* yet fully repented. Suffering, punishment, confession, remorse, and sorrow may sometimes accompany repentance, but they are not repentance. (*Ensign,* August 1988, p. 7.)

3. Repentance is not something that can be done piecemeal. We are not forgiven of our sins one at a time. Repentance is the process of turning our lives over to God. Repentance deals with all areas of our lives—not just a change of behavior in one area. When we are truly repentant, all of our sins are forgiven us and we are clean before the Lord.

What Repentance Is

1. Repentance is turning to God and placing him first in our lives. The very meaning of the word *repentance* is "a turning of the heart and will to God, and a renunciation of sin" (Bible Dictionary, LDS edition of the Bible, p. 760). We may stop smoking or go to church or begin to serve others for all kinds of reasons and not be repentant. When we do these things because our hearts are pure and we desire to do whatever God wants us to do, then we are repentant and will receive the forgiveness that we are seeking.

2. Repentance involves a total commitment to the Lord. We mentioned earlier that repentance cannot be accomplished piecemeal. This is because true repentance encompasses all areas of our lives. President Spencer W. Kimball taught the following:

> Repentance must involve an all-out, total surrender to the program of the Lord. That transgressor is not fully repentant who neglects his tithing, misses his meetings, breaks the Sabbath, fails in his family prayers, does not sustain the authorities of the Church, breaks the Word of Wisdom, does not love the Lord nor his fellowmen. A reforming adulterer who drinks or curses is not repentant. The repenting burglar who has sex play is not ready for forgiveness. God cannot forgive unless the transgressor shows a true repentance which spreads to all areas of his life. (*The Miracle of Forgiveness,* p. 203.)

3. True repentance is accompanied by a mighty change in our hearts. This change produces an abhorrence for sin and a desire to do good. After listening to King Benjamin, the Nephite people declared, "The Spirit of the Lord Omnipotent . . . has wrought a mighty change in us, or in our hearts, that we have no more disposition to do evil, but to do good continually" (Mosiah 5:2). The scriptures refer to this mighty change as being born again; indeed, our very nature is changed through the cleansing and transforming power of the Holy Ghost.

4. Repentance is doing our best. When we are repentant, we are not yet perfect but we desire to be. We do not excuse our imperfections but strive to improve and live all of God's commandments. Repentance is a sincere 100 percent effort, accompanied by the realization that God will help us grow as we do our very best. Talking to those who give excuses instead of effort, President Spencer W. Kimball wrote, "How can you say the door cannot be opened until your knuckles are bloody, till your head is bruised, till your muscles are sore? It can be done." (*The Miracle of Forgiveness,* p. 82.)

Elder Heber J. Grant explained the relationship between repentance, effort, and perfection when he said: "I do not believe that any man lives up to his ideals, but if we are striving, if we are working, if we are trying, to the best of our ability, to improve day by day, then we are in the line of our duty" (Conference Report, April 1909, p. 111).

5. Repentance involves godly sorrow. Sometimes people feel sorry because they were caught or because they caused loved ones to suffer or because they simply cannot sin and still be happy (see Mormon 2:13). These feelings are not godly sorrow; they neither demonstrate true repentance nor bring forgiveness. Godly sorrow comes from God through the Spirit and causes a person to desire to repent (see 2 Corinthians 7:9–10). President Benson discussed the importance of godly sorrow when he declared:

> Godly sorrow is a gift of the Spirit. It is a deep realization that our actions have offended our Father and our God. It is the sharp and keen awareness that our behavior caused the Savior, He who knew no sin, even the greatest of all, to endure agony and suffering. Our sins caused Him to bleed at every pore. This very real mental and spiritual anguish is what the scriptures refer to as having "a broken heart and a contrite spirit." . . . Such a spirit is the absolute prerequisite for true repentance. (*Ensign,* October 1989, p. 4.)

6. Repentance is possible because of the Savior. It is impossible for us to repent without his help, for none of us have the power to overcome our sins alone. Nephi clearly taught the importance of the Savior's help when he declared that "it is by grace that we are saved, after all we can do" (2 Nephi 25:23). Some Church members overlook the Savior's importance in the repentance process and feel we are saved or exalted by our works alone. In 1980, after interviewing many LDS members concerning their beliefs, *Newsweek* magazine stated:

> Unlike orthodox Christians, Mormons believe that men are born free of sin and earn their way to godhood by the proper exercise of free will, rather than through the grace of Jesus Christ. Thus Jesus' suffering and death in the Mormon view . . . do not atone for the sins of others. (*Newsweek,* 1 September 1980, p. 68.)

It is certainly wrong to believe that we are saved by grace no matter what we do, but it is just as erroneous to think that our works can save us. Without the Savior's suffering for our sins in the Garden of Gethsemane and without his ongoing help in changing our hearts and strengthening our will, we could never enjoy the sweet blessings of forgiveness, peace, and eternal life. We all have problems and weaknesses that cannot be conquered without divine help. As we cooperate fully with the Lord and do "all we can do," we place ourselves in a position to receive his help in overcoming our sins and becoming more Christlike. The Bible Dictionary in the LDS edition of the King James Bible explains the importance of grace in the repentance process:

> The main idea of the word is divine means of help or strength, given through the bounteous mercy and love of Jesus Christ.
>
> It is through the grace of the Lord Jesus, made possible by his atoning sacrifice, that mankind will be raised in immortality, every person receiving his body from the grave in a condition of everlasting life. It is likewise through the grace of the Lord that individuals, through faith in the atonement of Jesus Christ and repentance of their sins, receive strength and assistance to do good works that they otherwise would not be able to maintain if left to their own means. This grace is an enabling power that allows men and women to lay hold on eternal life and exaltation after they have expended their own best efforts.
>
> Divine grace is needed by every soul in consequence of the fall of Adam and also because of man's weaknesses and shortcomings. However, grace cannot suffice without total effort on the part of the recipient. . . . It is truly the grace of Jesus Christ that makes salvation possible. (P. 697.)

7. Repentance is usually a process, not an event. Actually, repentance is the process of becoming more spiritual—becoming more like God. Although a few people—like Alma the Younger and Paul—seemed to change in a matter of hours or days, most of us find complete repentance a lifetime pursuit, just as physical growth is generally slow and imperceptible. Only as we compare where we are now with the way we were a few years ago does our spiritual growth become apparent. Realizing this will help us avoid becoming discouraged in our spiritual efforts. As we continue to do our best to live the gospel and daily seek God's guidance and strength, slowly but surely we become more like him.

4

Faith

Our journey through life has been compared to a train traveling down a track at night. The engineer knows his desired destination. He also knows that a specific track will take him to that destination. Engulfed by the darkness, the engineer depends on the beam of light directly in front of the train. His view is confined to that beam. He cannot see what lies to the left, the right, or, perhaps more frightening, even straight ahead a mile or two down the tracks. All that he can see clearly is what is illuminated by the light on the front of the train. As the train travels further down the track, more of the view is revealed. If the engineer stops the train, he immediately stops revealing more track. But he continues on, confident that if he stays alert to what he can see and remains on the track, he will successfully complete his journey.

So it is with our life and the challenges we face. Heavenly Father has given us a clear track to follow to our desired destination. The way is clear, but we are allowed a totally clear view of only a short distance ahead. For the most part, the dark unknown of the future remains a mystery. We know that we must not stop but must keep going even though the unknown section of track might frighten us. We must have courage and faith to move further down the track. We must understand the major role that faith will play as we travel through our life's journey.

What Faith Is Not

1. Faith is not a perfect knowledge. Alma taught, "Faith is not to have a perfect knowledge of things; therefore if ye have faith ye hope for things which are not seen, which are true" (Alma 32:21).

The Lord gives us evidences that strengthen our faith and help lead us to things that are true. In Hebrews, Paul stated it this way, "Now faith is the substance of things hoped for, the evidence of things not seen" (Hebrews 11:1). He went on to say, "Wherefore seeing we also are compassed about with so great a cloud of witnesses, let us lay aside every weight, and the sin which doth so easily beset us, and let us run with patience the race that is set before us" (Hebrews 12:1).

Those experienced with flying will find significant meaning in Paul's use of the term *cloud of witnesses.* When you fly through a cloud, the cloud totally engulfs you. You can see nothing but cloud. Heavenly Father has engulfed us all with many witnesses or evidences of his reality and of the divinity of his Son. The universe and life upon this planet provide countless daily witnesses of God's power and glory. We have the prophets, past and present, that bear witness of God's goodness and reality. The scriptures serve as another powerful witness of God's plan and purpose for us all. Finally, we can each have the privilege of the Holy Ghost bearing individual witness to us. If we pay attention to these signs and witnesses and exercise faith in them, we will be surrounded with peace and knowledge.

2. The fruits of faith are not a free gift. Work and effort are required of us to receive the real fruits of faith. Ammon taught that the main fruits of faith are increased power with God and perfect knowledge. He taught King Lamoni:

I am a man; and man in the beginning was created after the image of God, and I am called by his Holy Spirit to teach these things unto this people, that they may be brought to a knowledge of that which is just and true;

And a portion of that Spirit dwelleth in me, which giveth me knowledge, and also power according to my faith and desires which are in God (Alma 18:34–35).

James taught that faith without works is dead (see James 2:17–18). It is by our effort that we show our faith in the things which God has revealed to us. Our faith must be tried before the fruits of faith can be borne. Moroni stated it this way: "And now, I, Moroni, would speak somewhat concerning these things; I would show unto the world that faith is things which are hoped for and not seen; wherefore, dispute not because ye see not, for ye receive no witness until after the trial of your faith" (Ether 12:6).

The brother of Jared was a great example of how this principle works. He followed the Lord's instructions in building barges to cross the waters but was unsure how his people would be able to see during the long journey in the ships' darkened hulls. When he went to the Lord to seek a solution to the problem, the Lord basically told him to figure out the problem himself. So the brother of Jared went to work on it by going into a high mountain, where he melted out of a rock sixteen small stones that were "white and clear, even as transparent glass." After he had done his part, he exercised his faith by going to the Lord with no doubt that he could lighten the stones with his great power (see Ether 3:1–6). At this point his faith turned to perfect knowledge as the Lord revealed himself to him:

> And because of the knowledge of this man he could not be kept from beholding within the veil; and he saw the finger of Jesus, which, when he saw, he fell with fear; for he knew that it was the finger of the Lord; and he had faith no longer, for he knew, nothing doubting.
>
> Wherefore, having this perfect knowledge of God, he could not be kept from within the veil; therefore he saw Jesus; and he did minister unto him. (Ether 3:19–20.)

The brother of Jared's experience teaches several important principles of faith, but one that we should always remember is to make our work the finest before God puts his touch on it.

3. Faith is not fear. Indeed, they are such opposing forces that Satan uses fear as one of his major tools. President Harold B. Lee taught: "The greatest danger among us today is fear. Fear doesn't come of the Lord. Faith and peace are the fruits of the Spirit." (*Improvement Era,* June 1970, p. 35.) Fear would entice us to stop the

train because we are not sure what lies beyond the lightened track. Faith would encourage us to continue our journey, knowing that even though the future events are unsure, if we remain on the right track we will have help in getting to our chosen destination. Elder Rex D. Pinegar gave the following counsel:

Do not fear the challenges of life, but approach them patiently, with faith in God. He will reward your faith with power not only to endure, but also to overcome hardships, disappointments, trials, and struggles of daily living. Through diligently striving to live the law of God and with faith in Him, we will not be diverted from our eternal course either by the ways or the praise of the world. (*Ensign,* November 1982, p. 26.)

We often fear that which we do not understand. As we study and live the principles of the gospel, our fear of life's challenges are turned to faith and hope in things to come. One of mankind's greatest fears is death. However, as we understand death and its purpose, we need not fear it. Elder Russell M. Nelson put it this way:

We need not look upon death as an enemy. With full under-standing and preparation, faith supplants fear. Hope displaces de-spair. The Lord said, "Fear not even unto death; for in this world your joy is not full, but in me your joy is full." (D&C 101:36.) He bestowed this gift: "Peace I leave with you, my peace I give unto you: not as the world giveth, give I unto you. Let not your heart be troubled, neither let it be afraid." (John 14:27.) (*Ensign,* May 1992, p. 74.)

Preparation is one of fear's greatest enemies. The Lord made this clear when he said, "If ye are prepared ye shall not fear" (D&C 38:30). Fear can be good if we use it as a catalyst to replace our fear with faith:

These three lines were lettered on the mantel in an English hotel at the time of Dunkirk, a time when every man or boy who could navigate, no matter how amateurishly, found a hero in him-self brave enough to help pursue England's army:

"Fear knocked at the door.
Faith answered.
No one was there." (Spencer W. Kimball, *Ensign*, July 1973,
p. 16.)

What Faith Is

1. Faith is letting go, as one family learned:

It was a family outing in the magnificent red-rock and blue-water country of Utah's Lake Powell, one of many this close-knit family had enjoyed. In one of the lake's lovely coves, the lure of the deep, blue water was strong. The motor was switched off, the houseboat drifted, and everyone went overboard for a swim.

"Everyone" included the family's 85-year-old patriarch. Never much of a swimmer but never one to be left out, he donned a bulbous orange lifejacket and slipped over the side.

The boat's boarding ladder had been lost—no problem for strong young arms and supple bodies when it came time to get back aboard. But for an 85-year-old it was a serious problem.

Grasping a tanchion, the patriarch struggled to climb aboard. Grown sons tried to push from below. Others tried to help from above, but his white-knuckled grip on the tanchion prevented effective help.

Finally, when his struggles had reached the point of despairing exhaustion, the plea of a daughter came clear:

"Dad! Dad! Reach up! Let go and reach up!"

It took faith, in his exhausted condition, to let go of that tanchion, but he did, and reached up. Strong hands grasped his wrist and lifted him into the boat.

"Thanks," he gasped as he sprawled on the deck. "I don't know how much longer I could have lasted."

And then, after a long, reflective pause, he seized the teaching moment:

"You know, I wonder how many times in my life I have struggled and relied on my own powers when what I needed to do was let go and reach up for help from above." (*Church News,* 16 November 1986.)

Faith requires our letting go of many things, including things we might think to be right, things we want, and things that are comfortable. In any case, we must have faith to let go and realize that the Lord knows what is best.

2. Faith is knowing that the Lord can do all things. Elder Loren C. Dunn taught:

Faith . . . is the realization that the Lord can help us with all things.

. . . Faith is the ability to do what we are prompted to do, when we are prompted to do it.

. . . Faith is the ability to live the laws of God that control the blessings we are in need of.

. . . Faith is the ability to act "as if."

. . . Faith is the ability to be charitable and to believe in people.

. . . Faith is the ability to allow ourselves to be guided by the priesthood. (*Ensign,* May 1981, pp. 25–26.)

5

Hope

What Hope Is Not

Hope is not merely a wish. The hope promised in the scriptures has a completely different meaning than the way the word *hope* is commonly used today. We hear people say that they hope someone is elected, or they hope they win the lottery, but these are merely wishes. This kind of hope is not based on experience or knowledge and is not accompanied with feelings of assurance but rather with doubt and uncertainty.

The hope the Lord promises us is often mentioned in conjunction with faith and charity and is much stronger than a mere wish. The Lord's hope is an expectation, an assurance of things to come. Most modern dictionaries indicate that hope is confidence in a future event, an expectation of something desired. It is the opposite of despair and fills the soul with courage, power, and peace.

What Hope Is

1. Hope is interrelated with and interdependent on faith and charity. Hope usually grows out of faith and leads to stronger feelings of charity. A writer once defined *faith* as feeling good about God, *hope* as feeling good about ourselves, and *charity* as feeling good about others (see Arthur R. Bassett, *Ensign,* April 1979, p. 9). Hope grows in our hearts as we come to realize that we are literally God's sons and daughters and that he loves us and wants to bless us. Our hope increases as we do the things God wants us to do, for we receive an assurance in our hearts that our lives are acceptable to him. As we begin to feel this hope—begin to feel better about ourselves and our relationship with God—we naturally begin to reach out and bless those around us. We begin to feel greater charity—the pure love of Christ—for all those we come in contact with. Hope is just as powerful and just as important to our spiritual growth as are faith and charity.

2. Hope springs from faith and righteous living. Faith in Jesus Christ and his atonement is an essential element of Christian hope. The Lord has promised us that our salvation is assured when we do what he says (see D&C 82:9–10). As our faith in the Lord and in his word increases and as we strive to live his gospel, our hope increases also, for we know that he will keep his word.

A faithful sister in the Church described the hope that comes when we understand the gospel and trust in the Lord in this way: " 'On August 3, my twenty-one-year-old son broke his neck in a diving accident six hundred miles from home. He hovers near death, but we are at peace. We do not understand the reason this had to happen, but we do understand the gospel.' " (As cited in Barbara W. Winder, *Ensign,* November 1986, p. 91.)

After reading this statement, Sister Barbara Winder, Relief Society General President, declared, "Let us recognize and be grateful for the blessings we have. From the Savior comes hope! Understanding the gospel, doing his works of righteousness, and following the counsel of our prophet are our *assurance* of the realization of that hope." (Ibid.)

3. Hope is an anchor to the soul (see Hebrews 6:19). It can surmount and vanquish tragedy, sickness, death, destruction, loneliness, and every other negative influence that may enter our lives. This facet of hope was clearly demonstrated by a Tongan stake Relief Society president named Lose Tafuna. Lose was a vibrant, enthusiastic young woman who loved and served the Lord with joy. She married a successful young man who had distinguished himself as a missionary and as a student. When they could not have children of their own, they were able to adopt and they continued to enjoy life together. Then serious disaster struck this loving and dedicated family. Lose's husband, Moli, suffered several brain tumors, which left him totally disabled. A friend of the family explained how Lose coped with this tragedy:

Moli Tafuna, bright, energetic, and dynamic, was now speechless, paralyzed, and completely helpless.

Watching Lose now, among a buoyant group of old friends who spoke energetically of children on missions, trips to the temple dedication, and prospective marriages, my thoughts were on her life of tragedy. For nearly five years now she had assumed the responsibilities of both father and mother and had been caring for Moli at home. Tonight, though, not a single line in her face betrayed the heartache she must feel. I marveled at her emotional stamina. After the food had all been served, I approached Lose to ask about her husband.

"Oh, he is doing just great. He is really wonderful."

"Can he speak at all?" I ventured.

"No, but he can communicate very well with his eyes. Just the other day, when I was about to give him his meal through the feeding tube, he raised his hand to say thank you. Oh, he's just great."

Lose seemed overjoyed over this feeble communication from her husband. Surely, I thought, this woman must yearn for companionship. Lose seemed to read my thoughts. She answered simply:

"It is enough to see his face." . . .

"Lose is constantly rejoicing that her husband is alive," explained Bishop Mahe. "Everything is a cheerful 'we.' She insists that I assess her a budget equal to the amount I would give them if her husband were still working at his old job at the airlines. 'We can do it,' she says.

"She is always eager," [Bishop Mahe] added, "to get home to see her husband. One would never know he was ill. She speaks of him as her greatest support." (Eric B. Shumway, *Ensign,* September 1984, p. 63.)

Brother Shumway closes his article with this statement about Lose. "Her love for [Moli] does not waver. She knows that in his emaciated bosom beats a burningly tender and thankful heart. She knows also that in eternity he will be completely whole and completely hers." Because of her faith and trust in the Lord, and her righteous living, Moli lives with peace and enduring hope rather than discouragement and despair.

4. Hope is a gift of the Spirit (see Romans 15:13). In the presence of faith and righteousness, the Spirit literally fills our hearts with hope. While serving as Primary General President, Sister Dwan Young's family experienced this great gift in their lives. The third child of their son Paul and his wife, Kathryn, was born with no passageway from her mouth to her stomach and was immediately flown by helicopter to a newborn intensive care unit in another city. Specialists decided that surgery was necessary even though Amy was only one day old.

The strain on this young family could have been overwhelming. Sister Young and her husband were in New Zealand, and Kathryn's parents were serving a mission in the Bahamas. Kathryn and her baby were in different hospitals in different cities, and their other two children, ages two and three-and-a-half, needed constant care at home.

The doctors successfully repaired the esophagus (the tube between the mouth and the stomach), but Amy developed pneumonia. After weeks of battling for her life in intensive care, medical experts determined that another operation was needed: whenever Amy fell asleep, she stopped breathing.

This difficult situation lasted for many weeks. Kathryn spent her days at the hospital watching her small infant struggle for her life. She and Paul met briefly at the hospital each evening as he came from work to spend the night there and she went home to take care of their other two children. Sister Young explained what helped the family through these trying times:

> What carried the family through this anguish? We never lost hope. Paul had given Amy a blessing as soon as she was born. He felt that all would not be well immediately and that they would have to put their trust in the Lord. We all knew that if we did all we could, we would have the courage to face whatever would come.
>
> That is the nature of hope. We do all we can, and then *the Lord stretches forth his hand and touches our lives with light and courage and, most of all, hope.* (*Ensign,* November 1986, pp. 85–86; italics added.)

Amy survived many months of respirators, hospital rooms, and close calls and is now a healthy three-year-old girl. Sister Young continued:

> And what if there hadn't been such a blessed outcome? Could we still go on with hope? Yes, because hope is knowing that whatever comes, the Lord can whisper peace. Our hope in Christ gives us an unchanging reason to rejoice. . . .
>
> The Lord wants us to be filled with hope—not just because it points us to a brighter tomorrow, but because it changes the quality of our lives today. *Hopeless* may be the saddest word in our language. Despair is the enemy of our souls. It can paralyze us, halt our progress, and cause us to lose our way. But hope awakens us like a light shining in the darkness. . . .
>
> We can endure all things when our hope is centered in one who will never fail us—our Savior, Jesus Christ, who is the light of the world. (Ibid., p. 86.)

When we are faced with obstacles that seem overwhelming, we can ask the Lord to touch our lives and fill our hearts with hope. As we place our trust in him and continue to keep his commandments, we allow the Spirit to enter and fill us with the peace, hope, and courage that we seek.

6

Charity

What Charity Is Not

1. $\mathbf{C}$harity is not just contributing to the poor. Paul made this very clear when he wrote, "And though I bestow all my goods to feed the poor, . . . and have not charity, it profiteth me nothing" (1 Corinthians 13:3).

Moroni defined charity as "the pure love of Christ" and indicated that it was the most important trait a person could acquire (see Moroni 7:46–47). He described what a possessor of charity would be like when he wrote, "And charity suffereth long, and is kind, and envieth not, and is not puffed up, seeketh not her own, is not easily provoked, thinketh no evil, and rejoiceth not in iniquity but rejoiceth in the truth, beareth all things, believeth all things, hopeth all things, endureth all things" (Moroni 7:45).

The pure love of Christ is an unselfish love—a perfect love. It is the type of love that Jesus showed for all of us when he suffered for our sins in the Garden of Gethsemane and then allowed himself to be nailed to the cross. Elder Bruce R. McConkie said that charity is a "love so centered in righteousness that the possessor has no aim or desire except for the eternal welfare of his own soul and for the souls of those around him" (*Mormon Doctrine,* p. 121).

This type of love was demonstrated literally hundreds of times by a man named Boyd Hatch:

> Deprived of the use of his legs, faced with a lifetime in a wheel-chair, Boyd could well have looked inward and, through sorrow for self, existed rather than lived. However, Brother Hatch looked not inward, but rather outward into the lives of others and upward into God's own heaven; and the star of inspiration guided him not to one opportunity, but to literally hundreds. He organized Scout troops of handicapped boys. He taught them camping. He taught them swimming. He taught them basketball. He taught them faith. Some boys were downhearted and filled with self-pity and despair. To them he handed the torch of hope. Before them was his own personal example of struggle and accomplishment. With a courage which we shall never fully know or understand, these boys of many faiths overcame insurmountable odds and found themselves anew. Through it all, Boyd Hatch not only found joy, but by willingly and unselfishly giving of himself, he found Jesus. (Thomas S. Monson, *Ensign,* December 1990, p. 5.)

2. Charity is not just a feeling. The attribute of charity is so powerful that it shapes all we say and do—the very way that we live. President Brigham Young alluded to this link between charity and performance when he said:

> Love the Lord thy God with all thy heart, and then speak evil of thy neighbor? No! No! Love the Lord thy God with all thy heart, and speak that which is not true? No, oh, no! Love the Lord thy God with all thy heart, and seek after riches of the world and forsake your religion? No! Love the Lord thy God with all thy heart and take his name in vain, curse and swear? No, never! If the love of God was really in the hearts of all who call themselves Latter-day Saints, . . . nothing would be sought after, only to build up the kingdom of God. (*Journal of Discourses,* 12:229.)

Our love for God and our fellowman will reveal itself whether at work, school, or home. The following story told by Elder Thomas S.

Monson illustrates in a very simple way this relationship between charity and our physical actions.

> A large and tough businessman, a wholesale vendor of poultry, showed his love with a single comment made when one attempted to pay for twenty-four roasting chickens. "The chickens are going to the widows, aren't they? There will be no charge." As he placed them in the car trunk, he said in a faltering voice: "And there are more where these came from." (Conference Report, October 1987, p. 82.)

What Charity Is

1. Charity is spontaneous. A couple who had recently moved missed many of the people and things they had left behind. While a visiting church leader was staying with them, he asked the wife what she missed the most and was told, "The roses. I miss my beautiful roses." A few days after the church leader departed, a delivery man knocked at her door with twelve rosebushes and instructions to plant them wherever she wished.

A missionary couple was assigned to a remote village in the Far East. One day, the wife commented to a family on how much she missed the fresh fruit they enjoyed at home. A few days later, one of the sons of the family stood at her front door with his arms full of fruit. She looked at the mountain in the distance, the only place the fruit could have come from, and said, "You went such a long way for this."

The boy smiled and said, "Long journey . . . part of gift." (See Joni Winn Hilton, *Ensign,* December 1990, p. 28.)

Such acts of kindness and love are not carefully considered and meticulously evaluated but arise spontaneously from hearts filled with charity. When we possess the pure love of Christ, we automatically and immediately respond to others' needs. Our actions are not based on selfishness, for charity "seeketh not her own."

Charity becomes our genuine disposition and permeates our whole personality. We do not love others because it is a duty or a command but because it has become our nature. Love becomes a spontaneous expression of how we feel about God and others. To withhold our desires to serve God and our fellowmen would be akin to trying to stop the flow of raging waters once they had broken through a dam.

2. Charity is impartial. One couple added six children to their family even though they already had two of their own. Three of these children came from Costa Rica, two from the Indian placement program, and one, a baby, they adopted in Mexico. They have worked hard to teach these children to love the beautiful brown skin that the Lord has given them. The following experience was shared by the adoptive mother of these children:

> One night in the bathtub, Trenton, age four, asked if I could wash him white. I was sure all my efforts had been in vain until a short time later.
>
> It was one of my low days. I was sitting in the front room looking out the window at the kittens playing on the lawn, and crying. Trenton climbed onto the chair and looked closely into my face. He asked, "Mom, are you mad at me?"
>
> "No," I answered.
>
> "Are you mad at Elisha?"
>
> I shook my head.
>
> "Then who are you mad at?"
>
> I told him I just didn't like myself very much today.
>
> He looked at me with his big brown eyes and said, "But you have to love you. Jesus made you that way. He couldn't make everyone brown. White is nice, too!" (Ronnell Jones, *Ensign,* September 1990, p. 27.)

This four-year-old boy is quickly developing an attitude of charity. Charity is not influenced or governed by such things as politics, race, economic conditions, or educational background. Charity causes us to offer our love to everyone and do all we can to help others.

3. Charity is a gift that God bestows on the righteous. Moroni said, "Pray unto the Father with all the energy of heart, that ye may be filled with this love, *which he hath bestowed upon all who are true followers of his Son, Jesus Christ"* (Moroni 7:48; italics added). Alma

taught the same thing in another way: "Bridle all your passions, that ye may be filled with love" (Alma 38:12).

Through righteousness and prayer, our hearts can be filled with love for God and for his children. Charity is a gift of the Spirit and is part of the process of being born again. As we receive and nurture this pure love of Christ, it enables us to live with him someday, for we become more like him (see Moroni 7:48).

4. Charity changes the lives of both the giver and the receiver. Joy, peace, friendship, contentment, and satisfaction are all natural byproducts of charity.

Several years ago, the Teton Dam broke, causing dangerous floodwaters to sweep through the Snake River Valley in southeastern Idaho. A member of the Church who was involved in this immense disaster shared the following experience:

> "I didn't cry when we saw our home ripped away from its foundation," he said. "I didn't cry when we thought of the photo albums and ordination certificates and irreplaceable personal treasures that would be gone forever. I didn't cry as we fought for everything we could save and repeatedly counted heads through the neighborhood to make sure lives were safe.
>
> "But later on, when I looked up and saw out of the night those buses and vans and jeeps and pickups rumbling toward us like an armored division of a heavenly army, I sat down and sobbed. Old people and young people and artisans and laborers—45,000 of them. They came from everywhere for hundreds of miles—over some roads still uncleared and unsafe. They tumbled out of those buses with shovels and buckets and hammers and food. 'It looks like you could use a hand,' they would say, laughing to keep back the tears at what they saw before them. Then shoulder to shoulder with friends I've never seen before and may never see again, we cleaned and sang and held each other up.
>
> "I cried then, and then only—not about the flood, but about what happened after it. I can't discuss it now without a lump in my throat." (As told by Jeffrey R. Holland, *Ensign,* April 1980, p. 28.)

We know some of those who volunteered to help during this disaster, and their lives are richer and more satisfying because of it.

Since charity is the very heart of the gospel, it only makes sense that it is a vital key to happiness, peace, and real joy. Ironically, many people seek happiness through gaining or getting something when it is unselfish giving that brings what they are really searching for.

Because of charity's eternal importance in our quest for happiness, it might be helpful to evaluate how we are doing by asking the following questions:

a. Do I enjoy serving others?

b. How much time do I spend in unselfish service?

c. Do I feel joy for others when they do better than I do?

d. Do I enjoy anonymous service?

e. Do I respect other people as individuals and allow them to hold opinions different than my own?

f. Do I allow others to make mistakes?

g. Do I condemn others when I find they have character traits I don't approve of?

h. Am I patient and kind with others?

i. Am I willing to forgive those who offend me?

7

Testimony

What a Testimony Is Not

1. A testimony is not a free gift. It begins with a small seed of belief and grows piece by piece according to our efforts and the grace of God. By carefully nurturing the seed through study, prayer, and righteous living, we can feel it gain strength as it grows and blossoms. President Ezra Taft Benson described the necessary elements to obtain and keep a testimony:

> I do not believe that a member of the Church can have an active, vibrant testimony of the gospel without keeping the commandments. A testimony is to have current inspiration to know the work is true, not something we receive only once. The Holy Ghost abides with those who honor, respect, and obey God's laws. And it is that Spirit which gives inspiration to the individual. (*Ensign,* May 1983, p. 54.)

2. A testimony is not a "thanktimony" or a travelogue. Too often the testimony meetings of the Church turn into a forum for expressing

gratitude or reliving experiences instead of bearing witness of the divinity of the Lord and his gospel. Elder Dallin H. Oaks expressed his concern when he shared the following:

> Latter-day Saints can become so preoccupied with our own agendas that we can forget to witness and testify of Christ.
>
> I quote from a recent letter I received from a member in the United States. He described what he heard in his fast and testimony meeting:
>
> "I sat and listened to seventeen testimonies and never heard Jesus mentioned or referred to in any way. I thought I might be in [some other denomination], but I supposed not because there were no references to God, either. . . .
>
> "The following Sunday, I again attended church. I sat through a priesthood lesson, a Gospel Doctrine lesson, and seven sacrament meeting speakers and never once heard the name of Jesus or any reference to him."
>
> Perhaps that description is exaggerated. Surely, it is exceptional. I quote it because it provides a vivid reminder for all of us. (*Ensign,* November 1990, p. 30.)

3. A testimony is not expressed in spoken words alone. Our actions must bear out what we say. For example, one man stood every fast Sunday and bore fervent testimony of the truthfulness of the gospel. During the days and weeks that followed, however, he would beat his children and belittle his wife with degrading and foul language. It is no wonder that the members of the community—and especially the ward—had a hard time believing that this man had a real testimony.

Conversion and testimony go hand in hand with words and action. James's counsel on faith and works could be changed to read: "Even so [testimony], if it hath not works, is dead, being alone. Yea, a man may say, Thou hast [a testimony], and I have works: shew me thy [testimony] without thy works, and I will shew thee my [testimony] by my works." (James 2:17–18.)

What a Testimony Is

1. A testimony is a spiritual conviction that Heavenly Father, Jesus Christ, and the Holy Ghost are real; that the Church was restored through Joseph Smith; and that God speaks through living prophets today. It grows when it is shared with others. In the Old Testament we read that after the Lord had sealed the heavens so there was no rain, he commanded the prophet Elijah to go to Zarephath to be fed by a widow. Upon arriving there he found the widow, who only had a handful of meal in a barrel and a little oil in a cruse. She and her son were about to eat what they thought would be their last meal when Elijah asked her to share of her remaining meal and oil. The widow was afraid to share but did so after Elijah promised her that she would not run out of either meal or oil. We read: "And she went and did according to the saying of Elijah: and she, and he, and her house, did eat many days. And the barrel of meal wasted not, neither did the cruse of oil fail, according to the word of the Lord, which he spake by Elijah." (1 Kings 17:15–16; see also verses 9–14.)

A testimony is much like the meal and the cruse of oil—as we share it with others, it will not waste away but will grow and increase in all ways. Not only was Elijah fed but so also did the widow and her son receive added food. So it is with sharing our testimony. Those who receive our testimony benefit, but we are also blessed by it. The Lord promised us: "Nevertheless, ye are blessed, for the testimony which ye have born is recorded in heaven for the angels to look upon; . . . and your sins are forgiven you" (D&C 62:3).

2. A testimony comes by small and simple things. Some might doubt that they really have a testimony because they have not had a heavenly visitation or some great miracle. Miracles occur and the heavens are opened to some, but neither are necessary to receive a testimony. The Lord counseled that "out of small things proceedeth that which is great" (D&C 64:33). By doing the small and simple things, we can build great testimonies. Daily going to the Lord in prayer, studying the scriptures, serving others, and keeping our baptismal covenants will bring, strengthen, and broaden our testimony. President Joseph F. Smith explained it this way:

It is not by marvelous manifestation unto us that we shall be established in the truth, but it is by humility and faithful obedience to the commandments and laws of God. When I as a boy first started out in the ministry, I would frequently go out and ask the Lord to show me some marvelous thing, in order that I might receive a testimony. But the Lord withheld marvels from me, and showed me the truth, line upon line, precept upon precept, here a little and there a little, until he made me to know the truth from the crown of my head to the soles of my feet, and until doubt and fear had been absolutely purged from me. He did not have to send an angel from the heavens to do this, nor did he have to speak with the trump of an archangel. By the whisperings of the still small voice of the Spirit of the Living God, he gave to me the testimony I possess. (Conference Report, April 1900, pp. 40–41.)

Elder Joseph B. Wirthlin counseled:

We should be patient in developing and strengthening our testimonies. Rather than expecting immediate or spectacular manifestations, though they will come when needed, we should pray for a testimony, study the scriptures, follow the counsel of our prophet and other Church leaders, and live the principles of the gospel. Our testimonies then will grow and mature naturally, perhaps imperceptibly at times, until they become driving forces in our lives. (*Ensign,* May 1987, p. 32.)

3. A testimony needs to be "serviced" regularly. Over the years we have learned that anything that is of any worth must be maintained. For instance, if we want our car to last for years, it must be serviced regularly. We must care for our homes with frequent repairs and paint as needed. Likewise our testimonies must receive constant attention, or they will dwindle and eventually die. President Harold B. Lee said: "A testimony is fragile. It is as hard to hold as a moonbeam. It is something you have to recapture every day of your life." (Harold B. Lee, *Church News,* 15 July 1972, p. 4.)

Servicing a testimony would include such things as daily communication with our Heavenly Father through prayer and scripture study, applying gospel principles through service to others, and keeping the commandments.

4. A testimony is eternal. When we were born into this life, we came with nothing; when we leave, we are allowed to take only a few precious gifts. President Ezra Taft Benson stated, "A testimony is one of the few possessions we may take with us when we leave this life" (*Ensign,* May 1982, p. 62). The time we spend nourishing and building our testimony is something that will be of eternal worth. Many have given their lives to share and preserve their testimonies. Two such individuals were Joseph and Hyrum Smith. They laid down their lives so that salvation could come to thousands. With regards to these two great men, we read in the Doctrine and Covenants the following:

> [Joseph Smith] lived great, and he died great in the eyes of God and his people; and like most of the Lord's anointed in ancient times, has sealed his mission and his works with his own blood; and so has his brother Hyrum. . . .
> . . . Henceforward their names will be classed among the martyrs of religion; and the reader in every nation will be reminded that the Book of Mormon, and this book of Doctrine and Covenants of the church, cost the best blood of the nineteenth century to bring them forth for the salvation of a ruined world. (D&C 135:3, 6.)

Most of us will not be called upon to give our lives for the sake of our testimonies. However, we are called to make choices that, if not made properly, could cost us our testimony. We must not only be willing to die but also to live for our testimony. Only through our testimony and faith in the Savior and his work can we obtain eternal happiness.

8

Reverence

What Reverence Is Not

1. **B**eing reverent is not the same as being quiet. A person may sit very quietly and not be reverent. On the other hand, a person may enthusiastically participate in an activity and yet feel and demonstrate deep reverence.

2. A person cannot be reverent at intervals. Reverence is a feeling about God, not an event that takes place and then is over. If a person is reverent on Monday and not on Tuesday, he probably was not truly reverent on Monday. Reverence is a feeling or attitude deep within our soul that does not change from moment to moment or from day to day.

This important principle was demonstrated during a young men's basketball game in a ward meetinghouse. On two different occasions during the game, one of the players ran over to the folding door separating the chapel from the cultural hall and crudely spit onto the folding door. After the second time, a spectator approached the coach of the boy and asked him to restrain the boy's spitting. This young man may have been quiet in the previous week's sacrament meeting, but he seriously lacked feelings of reverence. No one who feels reverence for God could spit on the walls of one of his meetinghouses.

3. Reverence is not limited to our thoughts and actions during meetings or in the Lord's meetinghouses. As we nurture the precious quality of reverence, we find that it affects our speech, prayers, dress, grooming, and relationships with others. It has a powerful influence on everything we do and everything we say.

What Reverence Is

1. Reverence is a deep respect for God. Because of the depth of feeling that is involved in true reverence, it is a difficult quality to define. President Spencer W. Kimball said, "Reverence has been defined as 'a feeling or attitude of deep respect, love, and awe.' " He went on to say that many Church leaders have described reverence as "one of the highest qualities of the soul, indicating it involves true faith in God and in his righteousness." (*We Should Be a Reverent People,* p. 1.)

Reverence includes respect, regard, esteem, and honor, and yet it is more. It begins with feelings deep in our souls that are so strong that they color everything we think and do. Reverence is homage and devotion; it is an emotion that leads to the realization that God is not to be approached nonchalantly or to be thought of lightly.

2. Punctuality is an integral part of reverence. When reverence is mentioned, most people's thoughts usually turn to behavior during meetings and in church buildings. Some irreverent behavior is easy to identify, such as children wandering in the aisles, adults and children talking with family or friends, people dozing, and parents not removing noisy children or babies from the meeting. However, there is other frequent behavior at church that is often overlooked. One such problem is the number of families who regularly disrupt the meeting by coming in late. Talking about this problem, President Kimball said:

> The home is the key to reverence, as it is to every other god-like virtue. . . . The last minute rush to gather the children, dress, and hurry to meeting is destructive to reverence.
>
> When families fall into this pattern they are frequently late to church, there are often cross words and hurt feelings, and the

children are often upset and restless during the service. How much more reverent is the family that prepares well ahead of time for meetings, that arrives at the chapel well before the meeting begins, and that sits together to listen to the prelude music and put worldly concerns out of their minds. (*We Should Be a Reverent People*, pp. 2–3.)

Even if families that come late are able to enter the chapel without distraction and immediately focus on the meeting, their tardiness is still a symptom that reveals a lack of reverence. When we remember that reverence is not just being quiet but is rather a deep feeling of devotion and respect for our Father in Heaven, we see clearly that reverence and habitual tardiness are opposites. Church meetings provide a place and time to worship God, a time when we convey our love to him and communicate with him through his Spirit. Tardiness to such meetings indicate rudeness and a lack of respect instead of love and reverence. Those who truly feel a reverence for God and take seriously their formal worship of him will not habitually be late in their appointments to do so.

3. Reverent feelings lead to proper dress and actions. We are a friendly people and love to visit with one another. Much of this visiting seems to take place before and after meetings in the chapel. Sadly, prelude and postlude music is often completely drowned out by the friendly noise and happy confusion in many of our chapels.

A lack of reverence is also displayed when we don't wear our best clothing to meet with the Lord, refuse to sing the hymns wholeheartedly, or fail to mention the Savior in our prayers and testimonies. True reverence always leads us to dress better, act better, and appreciate the Savior and his great sacrifice in our behalf.

The following excerpts are taken from a letter written by a nonmember. This woman had become impressed with the Church's teachings and attended several sacrament meetings with a member friend of hers. Notice the impact that the lack of reverence had upon this woman:

I was terribly disappointed at the lack of reverence in your chapel. Don't your people know just what and how much they have, so different and so much more truth than all the other churches? I was appalled and, yes, honestly disgusted at the noise and confusion during the service. Another thing that did not make a good impression on me was the boys who passed the sacrament—deacons, don't you call them? Some were even dressed in jeans, all colors of shirts, open at the neck, no ties. Not a very impressive sight for someone who had been led to expect differently. My friend asked me what I thought when we came out of the chapel. I told her it was almost like coming out of a hockey game. . . .

What a pity that the people who say they are members of the Church of Jesus Christ don't even know how to revere his name. (*Ensign,* April 1979, p. 74.)

The noise, confusion, and lack of proper dress are not as important as what they signify—the lack of a deep and profound respect for our Father in Heaven and Jesus Christ.

Honest feelings of reverence spawn attitudes of true worship that invite the Spirit of the Lord into our hearts. Elder L. Tom Perry tells a story that demonstrates this well:

Several years ago, I had the opportunity of traveling with the President of the Church to attend a series of area conferences. I will never forget the contrast between two conferences that were held just a few days apart. The first area conference was held in a large arena, and as we sat on the stand, we noticed continuous movement by the people. We saw individuals throughout the arena leaning over and whispering to family members and friends seated next to them. Giving the members the benefit of the doubt, we attributed the general lack of reverence to the nature of the facility.

A few days later, we were in another country attending another area conference in an arena much like the first. When we entered the arena, however, an immediate hush came over the congregation. As we sat through the two-hour general session, there was very little movement among the people. Everyone listened intently. Great attention and respect was shown all the speakers, and when the prophet spoke, you could hear a pin drop.

When the meeting was over, I asked the priesthood leaders

about what they had done to prepare the people for the conference. . . . The priesthood leaders explained that the reverence their people felt for God and His servants was the basis for their reverent behavior at the conference. (*Ensign,* November 1990, p. 71.)

4. Feelings of reverence increase as we fully participate in worship services. The important question is, if we do not feel this reverence for God, how can we develop it? One young man who lacked this reverence explained what he did to deeply change the way he feels about the Savior. He usually sat on the back row and goofed around with his friends, but one day he was late and there were no seats by his friends:

He sat alone, and for the first time in his life, he closed his eyes during the prayers, he sang the hymns, he listened to the sacrament prayers, and he paid attention to the speakers. About midway through the first speaker, he found tears welling up in his eyes. With some embarrassment, he carefully glanced around; no one else seemed emotional. He didn't know for sure what was happening to him, but the experience changed his life. It was during that meeting that he really started his spiritual preparation for his mission. He *felt* something, and fortunately, he acted and thus sustained those feelings. (Jack H. Goaslind, *Ensign,* May 1991, p. 46.)

Singing hymns of praise, listening carefully to the speakers and prayers, and considering the atonement of the Savior as we partake of the sacrament bring the Spirit into our hearts, which increases our love and reverence for God. Regular scripture study and personal prayer also increase our reverence for God and sacred things. As our reverence increases, we will find that we cannot take the Lord's name in vain or discuss his teachings or leaders in a negative way. Our love and respect for our Father will begin to affect how we feel about others, and we will draw closer to our families. As our reverence increases, our lives will become more rich and full, and the guidance and influence that we receive from the Holy Ghost will correspondingly increase.

9

The Scriptures

What the Scriptures Are Not

1. The scriptures are not boring. A young woman was lined up for a blind date by a friend. As the evening of the date progressed, she found her date to be charming and impressive. In their conversation that evening, she was surprised to discover that he had written a book she had recently read. The book had been boring and she had labored page by page until she had finished it. That evening, lying in bed, she thought about her date as she read the book again. The second reading proved to be totally different than the first. She found the book to be fascinating. She could hardly put it down. She wondered what had made the difference and knew that the only change was that she knew the author.

So it is with the scriptures. As we strive to know the author of the scriptures, they will take on new meaning and significance. What seemed boring can become interesting and helpful. Bishop J. Richard Clarke stated it this way: "Brothers and sisters, you don't have to be a natural student to read the scriptures; you just need to love the Lord" (*Ensign,* November 1982, p. 15).

A young man purchased a used computer without an instruction manual. He had worked on computers before and thought he had enough knowledge to use the computer without instructions. Hours of confusion and mistakes stacked on top of each other and brought discouragement. But the young man was stubborn and returned to his task time and time again, only to be met with more frustration. Anger turned to rage as he worked without success, until his wise father intervened and took him to a local computer shop, where they obtained the necessary instruction manuals. After all, who would know more about a complex computer than those who created it? Who would know most about its capacity and potential? Who would better know the safeguards required to avoid damaging or ruining the fine instrument? Soon the boy enjoyed his computer's full potential by following the instruction book provided by its creator.

Likewise in our lives, He who knows most about us, our potential, and our eternal possibilities has given us divine counsel and commandments in his instruction manuals—the holy scriptures. When we understand and follow these instructions, our lives develop greater purpose and meaning. We learn that our Maker loves us and desires our happiness. (See M. Russell Ballard, *Ensign,* May 1988, pp. 58–59.) As we understand who the Lord is and feel his love for us, the scriptures come to life and eventually become counted among our best friends.

2. The scriptures are not just for reading. Of course, "the scriptures that are never read will never help us" (L. Tom Perry, *Ensign,* May 1985, p. 23). We must first be willing to open and read the scriptures.

Can you imagine being away from home and receiving a letter from a loved one but not bothering to open or read it? This is similar to what happens when we don't read the scriptures. They are like letters from home telling us how we can draw near to our Father in Heaven (see Ardeth G. Kapp, *Ensign,* November 1985, p. 94). But we must do more than just read them:

Search the scriptures; for in them ye think ye have eternal life: and they are they which testify of me (John 5:39).

And now, whoso readeth, let him understand; he that hath the scriptures, let him search them (3 Nephi 10:14).

It is not by mistake that the Lord uses the word *search* when referring to the scriptures. Reading might be just a casual look, whereas searching is a careful study. If we want to gain a full understanding of what the Lord has to offer us, we must be willing to spend time carefully searching for the truths he wants us to know. Joseph Smith counseled:

Search the scriptures—search the revelations which we publish, and ask your Heavenly Father, in the name of His Son Jesus Christ, to manifest the truth unto you, and if you do it with an eye single to His glory nothing doubting, He will answer you by the power of His Holy Spirit. You will then know for yourselves and not for another. You will not then be dependent on man for the knowledge of God; nor will there be any room for speculation. No; for when men receive their instruction from Him that made them, they know how He will save them. Then again we say: Search the Scriptures, search the Prophets and learn what portion of them belongs to you. (*Teachings of the Prophet Joseph Smith*, pp. 11–12.)

3. The scriptures are not just for Sunday. All of us eat physical food each day. At times we nibble, at times we gorge, and almost always we make sure we have our three square meals. The same should be true when feeding our spirit on the words of God. We can set aside a time and place each day, even if it is just for a "nibble." Most of the time we can take the time to feast on and enjoy the words of God. As our spirits gain strength through regular nourishment, we will increase our ability to listen to the promptings of the Spirit. As that positive voice grows louder, it will muffle Satan's promptings.

Part of our daily experience with the scriptures should include what might be called pondering. Pondering doesn't have to be confined to our scripture study time; we can stop any time during the day to ponder on what we have read. This was explained by Elder Marvin J. Ashton when he said:

By pondering, we give the Spirit an opportunity to impress and direct. Pondering is a powerful link between the heart and the mind. As we read the scriptures, our hearts and minds are touched. If we use the gift to ponder, we can take these eternal truths and realize how we can incorporate them into our daily actions. . . .

We find understanding, insight, and practical application if we will use the gift of pondering. (*Ensign,* November 1987, p. 20.)

What the Scriptures Are

1. The scriptures are the standard by which all truth is measured. The standard used at the fruit stand to determine how much we owe is weight. The seller places the fruit on a scale and charges a monetary amount according to the weight of the fruit. The standard is the same for all customers, and everyone pays the same for a specific amount of fruit.

Likewise, the Lord has given us a standard by which we are to measure all truth. In the Church we call the Bible, Book of Mormon, Doctrine and Covenants, and Pearl of Great Price the standard works of the Church. They contain the standard by which we can measure all that we see, hear, and do. With regards to this, President Ezra Taft Benson counseled: "Always remember, there is no satisfactory substitute for the scriptures and the words of the living prophets. These should be your original sources. Read and ponder more what the Lord has said, and less about what others have written concerning what the Lord said." (*The Gospel Teacher and His Message,* p. 6.)

2. The scriptures are the Lord's voice to us. Think of someone you know well. Now listen in your mind as she talks to you. You can hear the pitch, the volume, the particular ways she has of saying each word. When you receive a note or letter from her, you can often hear her voice speaking to you as you read it.

Heavenly Father's and Jesus' voices are also known to us. We lived with them far longer than we have lived with anyone here in mortality. They have sent and continue to send letters to us through the scriptures and the teachings of the living prophets. These words can have both an immediate and a long-term effect on us. Jesus described it in this way:

And I, Jesus Christ, your Lord and your God, have spoken it.

These words are not of men nor of man, but of me; wherefore, you shall testify they are of me and not of man;

For it is my voice which speaketh them unto you; for they are given by my Spirit unto you, and by my power you can read them one to another; and save it were by my power you could not have them;

Wherefore, you can testify that you have heard my voice, and know my words. (D&C 18:33–36.)

3. The scriptures are fully understood only through the assistance of the Holy Ghost. Elder Bruce R. McConkie taught:

In the final analysis there is no way, absolutely none, to understand any scripture except to have the same spirit of prophecy that rested upon the one who uttered the truth in its original form. Scripture comes from God by the power of the Holy Ghost. It does not originate with man. It means only what the Holy Ghost thinks it means. To interpret it, we must be enlightened by the power of the Holy Spirit. It takes a prophet to understand a prophet, and every faithful member of the church should have "the testimony of Jesus" which "is the spirit of prophecy." (Revelation 19:10.) (*Ensign,* October 1973, p. 82.)

4. The scriptures are written for us. The Lord knows us by name; he understands our individual concerns and needs. Nephi counseled to "liken all scriptures unto us" (1 Nephi 19:23). We can do several things to make the scriptures personal. One way is to think about how we can personally apply the principles we are studying. As we do this, the Holy Ghost will enlighten our minds with applications to our individual lives.

Another way to personalize the scriptures is to mentally insert our own names in the scriptures as we read. For example:

For behold, I, God, have suffered these things for [your name], that [your name] might not suffer if [your name] would repent;

But if [your name] would not repent [your name] must suffer even as I;

Which suffering caused myself, even God, the greatest of all, to tremble because of pain, and to bleed at every pore, and to suffer both body and spirit (D&C 19:16–18).

We can also gain additional understanding by restating in our own words what we have read. By doing this, we are forced to think about what the passage means to each of us individually. As we use these and other methods of personalizing the scriptures, we soon find that they contain numerous practical applications for each of us.

10

The Mercy of God

A few years ago a Church teacher was discussing the importance of clean language when a young man in the class raised his hand and made the following statement: "You can't tell me that God will keep me from going to the celestial kingdom or make me suffer in hell just because I use a few bad words. Because God loves us, he is merciful. He might get after us and even punish us a little, but he will allow all of us to live with him again. After all, God is a merciful God."

Because this young man had no idea of what God's mercy is, he made some assumptions that may seriously affect his spiritual growth. Because he feels that the mercy of God will save him, he may not put forth the necessary effort to keep the commandments. Let's address several misconceptions that this young man and others have about mercy.

What Mercy Is Not

1. The mercy of God is not sympathy or pity. God does not save us just because he feels sorry for us or can't stand to see us suffer. He

does not want to see us suffer, but he is a God of justice as well as mercy.

2. The mercy of God is not a free gift of the Atonement. There are things that we have to do in order to qualify for blessings under the law of mercy.

Just because God loves us does not mean that he can exalt us. It is not within his power to take those who die in their sins and restore them to eternal life and a fulness of joy. God demonstrated his mercy by establishing a way so that we can return to live with him even though we have sinned. We can only partake of God's mercy as we follow his plan.

What the Mercy of God Is

1. The mercy of God is dependent upon Christ's sacrifice. In order to understand God's mercy and how it works, we need to understand two important laws: the law of justice and the law of mercy. The law of justice states that for every law broken, there is a penalty attached. That penalty is suffering; there are no exceptions. All broken laws lead to suffering.

God knew that all of us would sin. Because of his great love for us, he provided a way that we could avoid the penalty and return to live with him again. When we truly repent of our sins and turn toward God with all of our hearts, the law of mercy comes into effect. The law of mercy states that if we will sincerely repent, Christ's sacrifice atones for the sins that we have committed. Because of the great love that Jesus has for us, he was willing to suffer for our sins so we won't have to if we repent.

It is important to understand that someone has to fulfill the law of justice and pay the penalty for each sin—either Jesus or us. Jesus clearly explained this when he said: "For behold, I, God, have suffered these things for all, that they might not suffer if they would repent; but if they would not repent they must suffer even as I" (D&C 19:16–17).

When Alma's son Corianton committed the serious sin of immorality, Alma explained to him the relationship between the laws of justice and mercy. He said that because of sin "all mankind were fallen, and they were in the grasp of justice; yea, the justice of God, which consigned them forever to be cut off from his presence" (Alma 42:14). He then taught him that Jesus would atone for the sins of the world—"to bring about the plan of mercy, to appease the demands of justice"—so that God might be both a God of justice and a God of mercy (Alma 42:15). He summarized these laws by saying, "There is a law given, and a punishment affixed, and a repentance granted; which repentance, mercy claimeth; otherwise, justice claimeth the creature and executeth the law, and the law inflicteth the punishment; if not so, the works of justice would be destroyed, and God would cease to be God" (Alma 42:22).

The great mercy of God, then, is that he has given us an opportunity to repent by providing a Savior who suffered the penalty for our sins. Because he was sinless, he was not under the grasp of the law of justice and could suffer in our behalf. This redeeming gift of forgiveness does not come freely but is only offered to those who commit to follow Jesus and keep his commandments. Those who do not repent place themselves outside of the law of mercy and have to suffer the punishment for their sins. Thus, God is merciful in that he has provided a way for all of us to avoid the suffering for sin and to live with him again.

2. The mercy of God brings peace and forgiveness in this life. We learn to appreciate the beauty and importance of the law of mercy so much more as we see it applied in the lives of those we know and love. Elder Vaughn J. Featherstone related the following experience that he had while serving as a stake president:

> One day a woman came to my business office. She leaned across the desk and said, "President, I have carried a transgression on my heart for thirty-four years that I cannot carry one more step in this life. . . ."
>
> She said, "I know I will be cast out; I know I will be excommunicated, but does it have to be forever? Thirty-four years ago, before my first husband and I were married, I was involved in an abortion. Since that time, I have felt like a murderess. It was my husband's idea, and I did not resist. I had an abortion. Later we got married. He was unfaithful constantly during the first two years of our marriage. I finally divorced him and since remarried a

wonderful man who is a convert to the Church. He knows everything, and he still wants to be sealed to me. President, do you think that either in time or in eternity we can be sealed together? I know I will be cast out, but does it have to be forever?"

President Featherstone had known this woman for many years and considered her one of the most Christlike women he had ever met. His heart went out to her as she shared her confession with him. Because of the seriousness of the sin, President Featherstone wrote to President Kimball, then President of the Quorum of the Twelve, and asked him what should be done. After receiving President Kimball's response, President Featherstone called the woman into his office and read to her what President Kimball had written.

"Dear President Featherstone: You inquired about a woman who had been involved in an abortion thirty-four years ago. From the way you describe her it sounds like she has long since repented. You may tell her on behalf of the Church she is forgiven.

"After a thorough and searching interview, you may issue this sweet sister a temple recommend so she can go to the temple and be sealed to her present husband."

Elder Featherstone said, "If the Savior had been sitting where the woman sat, I would not have felt any closer to him. I believe that is exactly what he would have done. It was as though a two-thousand-pound burden had been lifted from the heart of this good woman. She wept great tears of relief and joy." (*Ensign,* November 1980, pp. 30–31.)

Consider the importance of the law of mercy in the life of this woman. She had been suffering for thirty-four years but, according to the Lord, had only tasted in "the least degree" the suffering that is attached to sin (see D&C 19:20). Because of Jesus' suffering, her heavy burden of guilt was replaced with peace. Even more important, if she continues repentant and obedient, she will never have to suffer for any of her sins in the life to come. Because of the great love and mercy that God the Father and Jesus have for us, we may enjoy this priceless blessing. It would be senseless to refuse this precious gift—a priceless gift that has already been purchased and is so lovingly offered.

11

The Priesthood of God

What the Priesthood Is Not

1. The priesthood is not for personal benefit and gain. Those who bear the priesthood might ask themselves when the last time was that they gave themselves a blessing or ordained themselves to an office. The answer is obviously, never. The priesthood is not for our personal use but for the benefit of others. The priesthood can only be magnified through service to others. Elder Gordon B. Hinckley described it this way:

> All of you, of course, are familiar with binoculars. When you put the lenses to your eyes and focus them, you magnify and in effect bring closer all within your field of vision. But if you turn them around and look through the other end, you diminish and make more distant that which you see.
>
> So it is with our actions as holders of the priesthood. When we live up to our high and holy calling, when we show love for God through service to fellowmen, when we use our strength and talents to build faith and spread truth, we magnify our priesthood.

When, on the other hand, we live lives of selfishness, when we indulge in sin, when we set our sights only on the things of the world rather than on the things of God, we diminish our priesthood. (*Ensign,* May 1989, p. 47.)

2. The priesthood is not imposing our will on others. The Lord instructed us concerning this when he stated:

When we undertake to cover our sins, or to gratify our pride, our vain ambition, or to exercise control or dominion or compulsion upon the souls of the children of men, in any degree of unrighteousness, behold, the heavens withdraw themselves; the Spirit of the Lord is grieved; and when it is withdrawn, Amen to the priesthood or the authority of that man (D&C 121:37).

Our use of the priesthood and our service under the direction of those who bear it and preside over us should always be in accordance with God's will, not ours. His will and bidding concerning the proper use of the priesthood come by way of the Spirit. It is imperative that we make ourselves worthy daily to receive the direction of the Holy Ghost. Elder Rex D. Pinegar made this clear:

A priesthood holder acts as a type of mediator between the people and God, representing them officially in worship and in holy ordinances. Because he represents God, he cannot take this office to himself but must be called of God. In a special sense, a bearer of this priesthood power and authority delegated by God belongs to God. He must be holy and clean before Him. He represents the Lord and acts as His agent when officiating in or performing his priestly duties. Such priesthood rights are inseparably connected with the powers of heaven and can, therefore, be handled or utilized effectively only on the basis of personal righteousness. (See D&C 121:36.) (*Ensign,* November 1985, p. 41.)

3. The priesthood is not something to be taken lightly. We all must honor and respect this great power, for it is of God. President Spencer W. Kimball described the respect and understanding that should accompany the priesthood:

The Lord has made clear that they who receive his priesthood receive him. And I think that means more than just sitting in a chair and having somebody put his hands upon your head. I think when you receive it, you accept it. You do not just merely sit. "And he that receiveth my Father receiveth my Father's kingdom; therefore all that my Father hath shall be given unto him." Can you imagine anything greater? Shouldn't we be frightened, almost awed as we contemplate the honor we have and the responsibility we have that has come from the oath and the covenant. (Stockholm Sweden Area Conference Report, 1974, p. 100.)

What the Priesthood Is

1. "The priesthood is the power and authority of God, delegated to man on earth, to act in all things for the salvation of men" (Bruce R. McConkie, *Ensign,* November 1977, p. 33). Those who hold the priesthood are called, ordained, and set apart to be agents for the Lord. The priesthood is God's power. Perhaps the greatest power that God has is the power to exalt his children. A child once asked the question: "What does God do for a living?" The answer to that question is found in the book of Moses: "For behold, this is my work and my glory—to bring to pass the immortality and eternal life of man" (Moses 1:39). Those who have been given the priesthood and called to serve under its direction have been "employed" by Heavenly Father to help in this work. Elder Bruce R. McConkie described it this way:

We can stand in the place and stead of the Lord Jesus Christ in administering salvation to the children of men.

He preached the gospel; so can we. He spoke by the power of the Holy Ghost; so can we. He served as a missionary; so can we. He went about doing good; so can we. He performed the ordinances of salvation; so can we. He kept the commandments; so can we. He wrought miracles; such also is our privilege if we are true and faithful in all things.

We are his agents; we represent him; we are expected to do and say what he would do and say if he personally were ministering among men at this time. (*Ensign,* November 1977, pp. 33–34.)

2. The priesthood always comes through authorized servants. Paul made this clear when he stated: "And no man taketh this honour unto himself, but he that is called of God, as was Aaron" (Hebrews 5:4). Aaron was called by God through Moses, who held the keys of the priesthood. God commanded Moses to confer the priesthood on Aaron and ordain him to a priesthood office (see Exodus 28:1). This did not happen just because Aaron thought he should have the priesthood—it happened through the proper channel of authority.

A fine man who had been ordained to the priesthood in another church was once asked where he got his authority to act for God. He gave the following explanation. As a young man he had served in the Air Force during World War II. He was assigned as a crew member aboard a bomber, and, while flying on a particular mission, the plane he was in was hit by the enemy and caught fire. He said that he got down on his knees and promised the Lord that if he saved his life he would serve him the rest of his life. The plane landed safely, and in his mind the sparing of his life was his call and ordination to serve God. No one would want to discredit the fact that God's hand was involved in saving this man's life, but it must end there. The Lord made it clear that the priesthood is his to give and that only he or his servants make the call. He told his disciples, "Ye have not chosen me, but I have chosen you, and ordained you" (John 15:16). This statement makes two things very clear about those who receive the priesthood. First, the Lord does the choosing through his authorized servants, and second, one must be ordained by those having the proper authority. Elder Boyd K. Packer taught:

The priesthood cannot be conferred like a diploma. It cannot be handed to you as a certificate. It cannot be delivered to you as a message or sent to you in a letter. It comes only by proper ordination. An authorized holder of the priesthood has to be there. He must place his hands upon your head and ordain you.

That is one reason why General Authorities travel so much—

to convey the keys of priesthood authority. Every stake president everywhere in the world has received his authority under the hands of one of the presiding brethren of the Church. There has never been one exception. (*Ensign,* November 1981, p. 32.)

3. The priesthood is eternal. The things of this world come and go. When we are faced with a particularly difficult problem in this life the statement "This too will pass" might come to our mind. How true that statement is of things that demand our attention in this life! Our jobs, homes, cars, bank accounts, and similar concerns will all pass away. All that will last forever will be God's children and the power and glory that he bestows upon them. The priesthood is the power by which the worlds are created and mankind is exalted. Whatever work is performed by or under the direction of the priesthood will not only have immediate influence but will also have eternal ramifications. Any work done by the priesthood is an eternal investment.

4. The priesthood is made operative by faith. As we exercise our faith, we will know of the power of God through his priesthood. Elder John K. Carmack taught:

The priesthood of God is potentially a greater source of power than electricity. Collectively, priesthood brethren perform well, but we fall far short of our potential. Why? Could our problem be that we fail to tap our greatest source of power in exercising our priesthood? Do we trade electricity for candles?

Faith in the Lord Jesus Christ is the priesthood's dynamic power source. By failing to put faith first in our callings, we reduce the priesthood's light and power. (*Ensign,* May 1993, p. 41.)

5. The priesthood is to be honored. A man was once honored for going fifty years without missing a Church meeting. When asked how he achieved such a great accomplishment, he simply explained that he had always been afraid that he might miss something the Lord had to give to him. This man's action showed that he had great honor for the Lord and his power.

Elder Russell M. Nelson gave us some do's and don'ts on how we might honor the priesthood:

Honoring the priesthood also means to honor your personal call to serve. A few do's and don'ts may be helpful:

• **Do** learn to take counsel. Seek direction from file leaders and receive it willingly.

• **Don't** speak ill of Church leaders.

• **Don't** covet a calling or position.

• **Don't** second-guess who should or should not have been called.

• **Don't** refuse an opportunity to serve.

• **Don't** resign from a call. **Do** inform leaders of changing circumstances in your life, knowing that leaders will weigh all factors when prayerfully considering the proper timing of your release. (*Ensign,* May 1993, p. 39.)

The greatest honor we can bring to Heavenly Father is to serve our fellowmen. We must always remember that the purpose of the priesthood is to bless the lives of God's children. When we do anything short of this, we dishonor the priesthood and him who gave it to us.

12

Sustaining and the
Law of Common Consent

What Sustaining and Common Consent Are Not

In July 1830, the Lord said: "All things shall be done by common consent in the church" (D&C 26:2). Since that time, many have misunderstood or abused this important gospel principle. Following are some of the misconceptions concerning sustaining and the law of common consent.

1. The law of common consent does not make the Church a democracy. The Church of Jesus Christ is the kingdom of God on earth. Notice it is a kingdom—not a democracy. It is governed by Christ, the Heavenly King. Elder Gene R. Cook pointed out that "we do not in the Church subscribe to a participative-management type of direction, wherein the opinions of all are gathered in, weighed and measured, a consensus drawn, and then a decision made according to the majority" (Conference Report, April 1978, p. 99). As members of the kingdom, we do not choose who shall lead us or decide what the doctrines of the kingdom will be. We only decide whether we will accept the decisions that the Lord has made in our behalf.

2. The law of common consent does not give us the opportunity to choose who will be our leaders. God makes these choices. We have the opportunity to sustain the leaders he has chosen and thereby receive his blessings and help.

If we vote against the counsel of those over us, we might do some slight harm to the growth of the Church and most certainly damage our own personal growth. One example of this happened approximately one hundred and fifty years ago at a special conference held on 7 October 1843. At this conference, President Joseph Smith expressed his dissatisfaction with Sidney Rigdon as his counselor in the First Presidency and asked the membership of the Church to release him. President Smith explained that Elder Rigdon had done nothing in his calling since their escape from Missouri, had participated in a scheme to defraud the innocent, and had been involved in a plot to arrest the prophet; he then added several other reasons why Elder Rigdon should be released from the First Presidency. Elder Rigdon then took the pulpit, refuted these charges, and asked the members to allow him to continue as a counselor to Joseph Smith.

Following Elder Rigdon's remarks, Joseph arose and expressed his entire lack of confidence in Elder Rigdon's integrity and steadfastness, but the members who were present voted to permit Elder Rigdon to remain as Joseph's counselor. Following this vote, President Joseph Smith arose and said, "I have thrown him off my shoulders, and you have again put him on me. You may carry him, but I will not." (See *History of the Church,* 7:47–49.)

Following this conference, Sidney Rigdon did nothing to build up the kingdom of God but instead worked toward his own financial benefit. When Joseph was killed, Sidney quickly returned to Nauvoo and claimed the right to lead the Church because of his position in the First Presidency. This caused much contention, and many members of the Church were led astray because Joseph's earlier counsel had not been sustained by the membership of the Church. Both individual and Church blessings were lost.

3. The law of common consent is not a means of validating a revelation. It only gives us the right to publicly raise our hands to the square and covenant with God that we will keep his word and do his will. If we refuse to sustain a revelation, it is still a revelation, but its attendant blessings of obedience are lost to us. Addressing this important principle, Elder Bruce R. McConkie wrote:

Revelation is revelation. When the Lord speaks, he has spoken. His word is to be accepted and obeyed if men expect to receive salvation. To reject the word of the Lord is to reject the Lord himself to that extent.

. . . It is as simple as that. The Lord's revelations are not submitted to man for his approval; they are revealed so that if man will obey them, he can gain an everlasting salvation in the kingdom of God. The Lord never designed that man would have the last word on his revelations. He, not man, is the Almighty. There is no scriptural warrant or authorization whatever for the view that the Church, its priesthood quorums, or any of its members, must vote to accept revelations before they become binding upon the Church members. (*Common Consent,* pp. 19–20.)

4. The law of common consent does not give us the right to vote against someone just because we don't like him. We are obliged to sustain those whom our leaders have chosen unless we know of a valid reason for declaring the person not worthy to serve. President Joseph Fielding Smith declared:

No man has the right to raise his hand in opposition, or with contrary vote, unless he has a reason for doing so that would be valid if presented before those who stand at the head. In other words, I have no right to raise my hand in opposition to a man who is appointed to any position in this Church, simply because I may not like him or because of some personal disagreement or feeling I may have, but only on the grounds that he is guilty of wrong doing, of transgression of the laws of the Church which would disqualify him for the position which he is called to hold. (Conference Report, June 1919, p. 92.)

There is also a proper way in which we might object. President Brigham Young indicated that we have the privilege of speaking our honest sentiments but emphasized that our objections should be expressed in the "proper time and place" to those in authority (see *Discourses of Brigham Young,* p. 148).

No good comes from backbiting or sharing our negative feelings with other members of the Church. If we know of a valid reason why a person should not serve, we should only share it with the presiding authorities at the proper time.

5. The law of common consent does not provide the right to vote anywhere or anytime. General Church business is voted upon by the general membership of the Church, stake business by members of the stake, and priesthood quorum business by members of the quorum. Only ward members have the right to vote on ward business. This principle applies to all of the organizations of the Church.

What Sustaining and Common Consent Are

1. Sustaining is much more than raising our arms to the square. It is doing everything we can to help someone serve successfully or to support a leader's decision. When we vote affirmatively, we covenant with the Lord that we will give our full loyalty and support. Sustaining means we will follow our properly chosen Church leaders, even if we don't understand why they want us to do something. The following story told by a stake president to Elder Richard L. Evans illustrates one reason why we should obey our leaders without equivocation or reservation:

> "I used to ride the range with my father, looking for lost sheep or cattle. And as we would mount a ridge we would look off into a distant hollow or a clump of trees, and my father would say, 'There they are.' . . . My father could see farther than I could, and often I couldn't see them. But I knew they were there because my father said so." (*Ensign,* December 1971, p. 59.)

Our leaders can sometimes see much farther than we can because the Lord has expanded their vision through revelation. As a matter of fact, we have sustained fifteen of our leaders as prophets, seers, and revelators, realizing that they can see things that have not yet been opened to our mortal view.

2. Sustaining is a sign of conversion. According to Elder Hartman Rector, Jr., "When we are converted, we sustain and follow the Lord's anointed servants; we find ourselves in agreement with them. Many

men with testimonies have been unable to do this," such as Martin Harris, David Whitmer, Oliver Cowdery, and Thomas B. Marsh. (See *Ensign,* May 1974, p. 109.)

3. When we accept and sustain God's leaders, we accept God and are accepted by him. Jesus told Joseph Smith that "he that receiveth my servants receiveth me; and he that receiveth me receiveth my Father; and he that receiveth my Father receiveth my Father's kingdom; therefore all that my Father hath shall be given unto him" (D&C 84:36–38). These promised blessings include peace, guidance, strength, and happiness here upon the earth, and eternal life and a fulness of joy in the world to come.

13

Tithing

What Tithing Is Not

1. Giving less than ten percent is not tithing. President Lorenzo Snow stated: "A part of a tithing is no tithing at all, no more than immersing only part of a person's body is baptism" (*The Teachings of Lorenzo Snow*, pp. 155–56). Some ask the question, "What is an honest tithing?" The Lord clarified what he requires when he declared: "And after that, those who have thus been tithed shall pay one-tenth of all their interest annually; and this shall be a standing law unto them forever, for my holy priesthood, saith the Lord" (D&C 119:4).

Many wonder what the Lord meant by the term *interest*. Elder Howard W. Hunter described it as follows:

> The law is simply stated as "one-tenth of all their interest." Interest means profit, compensation, increase. It is the wage of one employed, the profit from the operation of a business, the increase of one who grows or produces, or the income to a person from any other source. The Lord said it is a standing law "forever" as it has been in the past. (*Improvement Era*, June 1964, p. 276.)

Anything short of what the Lord requires is not considered an honest tithe. It isn't always easy to pay an honest tithing, and some try to justify doing something less. Malachi went as far as to say that anything less than an honest tithe is robbery (see Malachi 3:8–9). Elder Howard W. Hunter compared it to the crime of embezzlement. He first defined embezzlement as property that belongs to another and that which is acquired lawfully but then fraudulently converted to the possessor's use. The nontithepayer is committing the crime of embezzlement against the Lord. He takes the Lord's share, which came into his hands lawfully, but misappropriates it for his own use. (See *Improvement Era,* June 1964, p. 276.)

If a person is not sure what an honest tithing is, it would be wise to consider the following:

> When you are in doubt as to just how you should calculate your tithes, reverse the terms as we sometimes do in solving complex mathematical problems and suppose for the time being that the Lord had said this; let us postulate this is an assumed law given to the Church: "In order to show my love for my people, the faithful members of my Church, it is my will, saith the Lord, that each one shall receive from my storehouse, the storehouse of my Church, at regular intervals during the year, an amount equal to one-tenth of his income." Now . . . sit down and calculate how much the Lord owes you under that kind of law, and then go pay it to your bishop. (James E. Talmage, Conference Report, October 1928, p. 119.)

If we are to err in paying our tithing, let the error be in God's favor. Elder George Q. Cannon taught: "I urge with all my heart that all the members of this Church who should pay tithing, pay an honest tithing—and don't scrape the measure off too level. Put a little offering of gratitude there, to heap things up until they are running over with the blessings we receive from him." (*Improvement Era,* June 1953, pp. 435–36.)

2. Tithing is not the door to worldly riches. Sometimes we misinterpret Malachi's promise of the windows of heaven being opened to mean that we will become rich. Elder Gordon B. Hinckley taught: "Now, do not get me wrong. I am not here to say that if you pay an honest tithing you will realize your dream of a fine house, a Rolls

Royce, and a condominium in Hawaii. *The Lord will open the windows of heaven according to our need, and not according to our greed." (Ensign,* May 1982, p. 40.)

The Lord's blessings to those who pay an honest tithing are far greater than worldly riches. Elder N. Eldon Tanner explained it this way: "If we obey this commandment [tithing], we are promised that we will 'prosper in the land.' This prosperity consists of more than material goods—it may include enjoying good health and vigor of mind. It includes family solidarity and spiritual increase." (*Ensign,* November 1979, p. 81.)

Similarly, President Heber J. Grant stated:

> Prosperity comes to those who observe the law of tithing; and when I say prosperity I am not thinking of it in terms of dollars and cents alone . . . ; but what I count as real prosperity, . . . the growth in a knowledge of God, a testimony, and the power to live the gospel and to inspire our families to do the same. That is prosperity of the truest kind. (Conference Report, April 1925, p. 10.)

What Tithing Is

1. Paying tithing is an exercise in faith. When a person makes the choice not to pay tithing, he has openly made the choice not to exercise faith in God and his promises. For many others, however, the choice to pay tithing requires a great deal of faith.

Elder Angel Abrea tells of such faith. As a new branch president in Argentina, he decided to interview the members of the branch with respect to the importance of paying tithing. He found himself talking to a good brother who had difficulty paying his tithing. He asked him bluntly, "Brother Jose, why don't you pay your tithing?" After a moment of silence, Jose responded: "As you know, President, I have two children. The wage of a laborer is very low. This month I have to buy my children shoes to go to school; and, mathematically, I just don't have enough money."

In an instant response Elder Abrea said, "Jose, I promise you that if you pay your tithing faithfully, your children will have their shoes to go to school, and you will be able to pay for all the needs of your home. I don't know how He will do it, but the Lord always keeps his promise. Besides that, if you still find that you don't have enough money, I will give you back what you paid in tithing from my own pocket."

On the way home, he wondered if what he had done was the right thing. He was recently married, just getting started in his career, and faced with his own economic problems. He began to worry about his own shoes, let alone those of Jose's family!

When he arrived home, his wife assured him that he had done the right thing and that everything would be all right. That night he offered a fervent prayer in Jose's behalf.

One month later, he again sat down with Jose. Though the tears in his eyes almost made it impossible for him to speak, Jose said: "President, it is incredible. I paid my tithing; I was able to meet all of my obligations, and I even purchased the new shoes for my children, all without an increase in my wage. I know that the Lord keeps his promises!" (See Conference Report, October 1981, p. 34.)

Elder George Q. Cannon summarized this principle when he stated: "I think when people say they haven't money enough to pay tithing, they should say they haven't faith enough to pay tithing" (*Improvement Era*, June 1953, p. 453).

2. Tithing is a debt owed to God. All that we have has been given to us by Heavenly Father. It is vital therefore that we recognize his hand in all that he has blessed us with. In the Doctrine and Covenants the Lord stated:

> And it pleaseth God that he hath given all these things unto man; for unto this end were they made to be used, with judgment, not to excess, neither by extortion.
>
> And in nothing doth man offend God, or against none is his wrath kindled, save those who confess not his hand in all things, and obey not his commandments. (D&C 59:20–21.)

It is very offensive to God when we fail to pay an honest tithe. Elder Howard W. Hunter explained:

> The Lord has established the law of tithing, and because it is his law, it becomes our obligation to observe it if we love Him and

have a desire to keep his commandments and receive his blessings. In this way it becomes a debt. The man who doesn't pay his tithing because he is in debt should ask himself if he is not also in debt to the Lord. The Master said: "But seek ye first the kingdom of God and his righteousness: and all these things shall be added unto you." (Matt. 6:33.) (*Improvement Era,* June 1964, p. 276.)

3. Tithing is for everyone. Regardless of our age or circumstance in life, the payment of tithing is not only an obligation but a privilege for each of us.

President Spencer W. Kimball remembered being taught at a very young age the importance of tithing as his mother took eggs to the bishop's house. He also never forgot his father's counsel during haying time: " 'The best hay is on the west side of the field. Get your load for the tithing barn from that side. And load it full and high.' " On another occasion Andrew Kimball counseled Spencer and his sister Alice: " 'The Lord has been kind to us. We planted and cultivated and harvested, but the earth is the Lord's. He sent the moisture and the sunshine. One-tenth we always give back to the Lord for his part.' " These teachings left such an impression on Spencer that he observed: "Pa made no requirement . . . , he merely explained it so convincingly that we felt it an honor and privilege to pay tithing." From these great lessons, President Kimball learned to pay tithing at a young age and to view it as a great privilege and honor. (See *Spencer W. Kimball,* pp. 31–32.)

President Joseph F. Smith related a vivid circumstance that occurred in the days of his childhood. His mother was a widow with a large family to provide for. One spring when they opened their potato pits, she had her boys get a load of the best potatoes, which she took to the tithing office. Potatoes were scarce that season. President Smith was a little boy at the time and drove the team. When they drove up to the steps of the tithing office, one of the clerks, named William, came out and said to his mother, "Widow Smith, it's a shame that you should have to pay tithing." He went on to chide her for paying her tithing, called her anything but wise or prudent, and said there were others who were strong and able to work who were supported from the tithing office. President Smith's mother then turned on him and said: "William, you ought to be ashamed of yourself. Would you deny me a blessing? If I did not pay my tithing, I should expect the Lord to withhold his blessings from me. I pay my tithing, not only because it is a law of God, but because I expect a blessing by doing it. By keeping this and other laws, I expect to prosper, and to be able to provide for my family." (See *Gospel Doctrine,* pp. 228–29.)

The law of tithing has been given to us for the benefit of all the Saints in God's kingdom. If we are all united in paying an honest tithing, many great things can happen to further God's work here on earth.

14

Home Teaching and Visiting Teaching

Rather than mentioning both home and visiting teaching every time a principle is discussed in this chapter, we decided to refer to home teaching only. Although a few principles apply strictly to home teaching, most apply to visiting teaching as well. However, we have used visiting teaching and home teaching statements and stories throughout so that all may benefit.

What Home Teaching Is Not

1. Home teaching is not visiting a home once a month. A frequently told story concerns a stake president who was kindly rebuking an elders' quorum president for his quorum's home teaching percentage. The quorum president interrupted him and explained that it was impossible to do home teaching during the months of October and December. When the surprised stake president asked him to explain, he was reminded that both October and December ended in holidays: "Since it would be rude to visit our assigned families on a holiday, we simply can't do home teaching during these two months."

President Spencer W. Kimball effectively destroyed the myth that home teaching was a monthly visit when he said:

Whenever I think of visiting teachers, I think of [home] teachers also, and think that certainly your duties in many ways must be much like those of the [home] teachers, which briefly are "to watch over the church always"—not twenty minutes a month but always—"and be with and strengthen them"—not a knock at the door, but to be *with* them, and *lift* them, and strengthen them, and empower them, and fortify them—"and see that there is no iniquity, . . . neither hardness, . . . backbiting, nor evil speaking." (D&C 20:53–54.) (*Ensign,* June 1978, p. 24.)

2. Home teaching is not just becoming friends. There is no doubt that becoming friends is vital to our success as home teachers, but it is only the first step. Successful home teachers strive to help their families grow, and they look for ways that they can build and fortify them and help them in meeting their needs. After discussing the importance of helping our families become more like God, President Kimball said:

Don't let us be satisfied with just visits, with making friends; that, of course, has its place. With our missionary program, we constantly have that to consider. Sometimes a missionary gets it in his head that he has got to build a great bridge, and so he builds ten or twenty or thirty miles of approach to get over a quarter mile of bridge. He is worn out by the time he gets to the bridge, and then he has difficulty doing his job. Friendship, of course, is important, but how better can you make a friend than to teach somebody everlasting principles of life and salvation? (*Ensign,* June 1978, p. 25.)

What Home Teaching Is

1. Home teaching is a basic responsibility of priesthood holders. In a message to the Priesthood Home Teaching Committee of the

Church in July 1966, Elder Marion G. Romney stated: "No man can magnify his calling in the priesthood and refuse to do home teaching." Even men as busy as Presidents N. Eldon Tanner and Marion G. Romney served as home teachers while they served as counselors to President Kimball. Whether we are called to any other position in the Church, all of us have an opportunity and a responsibility to assist in this great work. President Ezra Taft Benson emphasized the importance of home teaching when he declared: "There is no greater Church calling than that of a home teacher. There is no greater Church service rendered to our Father in Heaven's children than the service rendered by a humble, dedicated, committed home teacher." (*Ensign,* May 1987, p. 50.)

2. Home teaching is a special and sacred opportunity, not a dreadful responsibility. When we approach home teaching with the proper attitude, great things happen. Referring to this opportunity, President Kimball said: "There are many sisters who are living in rags—spiritual rags. They are entitled to gorgeous robes, spiritual robes, as in the parable. It is your privilege more than your duty. We talk so much about duty, but it is your privilege to go into homes and exchange robes for rags." (*Ensign,* June 1978, p. 26.)

We can approach home teaching the way Laman and Lemuel approached their responsibilities, or we can follow in Nephi's footsteps. When Lehi asked Laman and Lemuel to return to Jerusalem and obtain the brass plates, they murmured and claimed that it was a hard thing the Lord wanted them to do (see 1 Nephi 3:5–6).

When Nephi was approached, he said, "I will go and do the things which the Lord hath commanded" (1 Nephi 3:7). Because of his willing attitude and his trust in the Lord, Nephi was successful in helping many people gain eternal life. The consequences of Laman and Lemuel's constant criticism and faithlessness was that they not only failed to help others but also led thousands of people astray, including their own posterity.

Nephi taught us that the Lord will always prepare a way so that we can accomplish what he asks us to do (see 1 Nephi 3:7). As we accept our home teaching call with faith, fill it with enthusiasm, and seek the Lord's guidance, he will help us to bless the lives of our assigned families.

3. One of our most important home teaching goals is to bring

people to Christ. After mentioning home teachers and visiting teachers, Elder Henry B. Eyring declared, "None of the people for whom you are responsible can be truly served without your bearing testimony, in some way, of the mission of Jesus Christ" (*BYU 1989–90 Devotional and Fireside Speeches,* p. 41). Amid the landslide of meetings and responsibilities, we sometimes lose our direction. However, bringing people to Christ should be the main goal of all of our church service. Elder Gene R. Cook explained this in more detail when he said:

> We do not visit the active just to "visit," or the less active just to get them out to church, although that may be part of what happens. In essence, we visit to help the heads of those homes, male or female, to become the spiritual leaders in their homes, to lead their families to Christ, to pray, to fast, and to read the scriptures together. If that happens in our visits, all else will take care of itself. (*Ensign,* November 1988, pp. 37–38.)

4. Home teaching helps us focus our desire to serve others. Most of us want to give compassionate service, but we sometimes feel hesitant because we don't know what others need or how to approach them. Home teaching helps solve this problem, for we have specific opportunities to get to know our families well and help them in ways that will matter most. This facet of home teaching was illustrated by a woman who had recently moved into a new ward. She enjoyed the ward but didn't feel the love and compassion that she had enjoyed in her previous ward.

One day she called a member of the Relief Society presidency and volunteered to help anywhere she might be needed. When the counselor told her the names of three women in the ward who needed help, she was surprised and humbled—the counselor had unknowingly named three of the sisters she was assigned to visit as a visiting teacher. (See Susan Roylance, "Sharing," *Ensign,* August 1980, p. 61.)

This sister came to realize that her desire to give service and build love could be fulfilled as she performed her own visiting teaching assignment.

5. Home teaching is a training process for junior companions. Through their association with faithful priesthood brethren, young

men can learn how to magnify their priesthood and bless others' lives. For many young men who come from homes without a positive priesthood example, this can be vital to their spiritual growth and eternal future.

In many cases, less-active members are coupled in a home teaching relationship in order to help them grow spiritually. This was the case with a young man named Derek. He had been active throughout his teen years, but when he refused a mission call, he began to feel that his family and the ward members were disappointed with him. His church attendance slipped, and his attitude toward the Church began to sour.

Even though he was not an elder, he attended the elders quorum meetings on his occasional visits to church. He was really surprised when he was asked to be a home teacher with a friend whom he had known throughout his life. He was in the process of planning how to avoid his call when his new partner came up and said, "Why don't we show the guys in our ward how home teaching should really be done?" This appealed to Derek because he felt this would show others that he wasn't as bad as they thought he was.

As the two home teachers met with the fathers of their assigned families, one father asked them to share stories from the Book of Mormon with his family. Since Derek's companion was going on a mission in three months, he suggested that they come several times a month so they could finish the Book of Mormon before he left.

As the home teachers met with this family, there was such a sweet spirit present that Derek began to really read and study the Book of Mormon so that he wouldn't disappoint the family. Within the next two months he read the entire Book of Mormon, and a great change began to take place in his heart. Eric explained what happened next:

> Suddenly, I knew the Book of Mormon was true! The seed of faith had been planted within me, and now it had grown until I could scarcely contain it. I wanted to tell everyone I met of the joy I felt in finding out that the Book of Mormon was true, that Joseph Smith was indeed a prophet of God, and that the teachings of The Church of Jesus Christ of Latter-day Saints were true. I wept in gratitude for having received this witness.
>
> I drove over to Bishop Toolson's house and knocked on the

door. He answered, invited me in, and asked what he could do for me. . . . The words burst from me: "I want to go on a mission." (Derek Preece, *Ensign,* September 1990, pp. 20–21.)

Because of a dedicated and inspired home teaching companion, Derek's life was changed. When this story appeared in the *Ensign,* he was serving as a counselor in his ward bishopric.

One of the most important benefits of home teaching is the opportunity to help our companion draw closer to God and learn how to honor the priesthood.

6. Home teaching works! It works because it is the Lord's program. When we seek the Lord's guidance and follow the principles that have been taught by our leaders, lives can be changed and souls saved.

John Linton exemplified this type of home teaching. At his funeral his bishop shared the following story:

Brothers and sisters, I was one of those who had been lost to the Church. I fought against the truth with bitter passion until the man we honor today befriended me. He could well have been my father, though our ages were only a few years apart. He came to my house as a home teacher and listened to my bitter accusations. He listened until I had no more to say, and then he said he understood why I felt the way I did. He continued to come with love that never condemned and patience that was never exhausted. I don't remember how it all began, but gradually I found myself listening to him. I anticipated his visits, for he always said the things I needed to hear. The time came when I pondered his words for days and could not rid my mind of their implications. There were dark hours of personal struggle and intense remorse—and still he came to help me somehow make amends for my misdirected life. I prayed, and he prayed with me; I wept, and he wept with me; I rejoiced, and he rejoiced with me. I sometimes wonder if he ever sensed that Boyd Johnson, a bitter and hopeless man, could be sufficiently changed to become his bishop. Whether he knew or not, I thank God that he followed the promptings of the Spirit, for a miracle came about in my life. I revere the name of John Linton, for through his love, those words spoken of the Prodigal Son have come to apply to me, "For this my son was dead, and is alive again; he was lost, and is found." (Luke 15:24.) (*To Make Thee a Minister and a Witness,* p. 113.)

John Linton listened to and followed the Spirit—and a life was forever changed. Obedience, patience, compassion, and love led to the salvation of another soul. Prayer, sorrow, and joy were shared, and two men became eternal friends. Thousands of home teachers can testify of experiences similar to this one. The home teaching program really does work when we work the program. Home teaching and visiting teaching are the very backbone of activation and compassionate service in the Lord's church.

15

Opposition and Suffering

Tony was born with a disease called arthrogryposis, which, although not life threatening, left his limbs virtually useless. To make matters worse, he was abandoned by his parents when they learned of his condition. When he was six months old, he was taken in by a family of five and later adopted. Without the use of arms to reach what he wanted or hands to clench his toys, he developed amazing coordination with his mouth and neck. With his parents and family emphasizing the need for education, it was imperative that Tony learn to write legibly. This in itself was an accomplishment that his own doctors said would be impossible.

Like most first graders, he was soon bringing home stick figures and crude drawings of family members and pets. As abstract as most six-year-olds' drawings, these were his sole outlet for expression and entertainment.

The early values taught by his parents gave him a desire to make his way through life with whatever talents he could develop. While Tony's sister and two brothers took on the normal after-school activities, he buried himself into practicing his drawing by the hour. This practice led him to his life work. Today he earns his own way as an accomplished artist.

His achievements were not only focused on art. Tony and his

brother Rick became closer than most brothers hope to be. Together they soon developed ways to expand Tony's horizons to include such things as table tennis, bowling, and even weight lifting. (Tony managed to lift one hundred and ten pounds with his mouth!) Later they were also able to go deep-sea fishing together. Of course, it wasn't enough for Tony to simply ride along on Rick's charter boat. Soon they were competing in Florida tarpon and kingfish tournaments where the quarry often outweighs the competitors. With Rick at the helm and Tony clenching the reel handle in his teeth, they were soon adept at boating fish over one hundred pounds.

It would seem that Tony had met and overcome great opposition and suffering in his life. But for him there was one question that went unanswered. He wondered why he was born the way he was. He had great faith that there was a God, so he sought an answer by asking people who seemed to be religious. He usually got one of two answers. One was that God knew he was going to be a sinner, so he gave him a deformed body to try and stop him from sinning. The other was that his handicap was his punishment for being a sinner.

You can imagine the disgust and lack of peace that Tony must have felt. Then one day Tony met a woman from one of the local newspapers who came to his home to do an article on him. This wonderful Latter-day Saint helped Tony realize that the answers he had received to his question were just what Tony thought they were—garbage.

She first helped him understand that he was asking the wrong question. Instead of asking, "Why has this happened to me?" he should have asked, "God, what is it that you want me to learn from this?" Once Tony started asking that question, his life took on a new meaning. With patience and practice, his art continued to develop until the intricate designs and pictures drew many to marvel at their beauty. Regarding his great success despite his physical handicaps, he said, "I feel that the Lord is the one that gives everyone a means or a talent to earn their own way in life. I know that God gave me a gift to draw in my heart, although I'm unable to use my arms or legs. My desire and faith in the Lord guided me to develop this skill of drawing with my mouth. One of my purposes in this world might be to show people that no matter how discouraging things seem, you can still accomplish it with determination and faith in the Lord's help."

What Opposition and Suffering Are Not

We learn some really important things from Tony's experience about opposition and suffering.

1. Opposition and suffering are not bad. Some of the greatest growth we will ever have in life comes because of the trials we must bear. Just as muscles need resistance to grow and become strong, so are the characters of mankind. President Spencer W. Kimball, who knew well the sufferings of life, stated:

Is there not wisdom in his giving us trials that we might rise above them, responsibilities that we might achieve, work to harden our muscles, sorrows to try our souls. Are we not permitted temptation to test our strength, sickness that we might learn patience, death that we might be immortalized and glorified? (*The Teachings of Spencer W. Kimball*, p. 39.)

2. The individual trials we face should not be considered punishment from God. Many of our difficulties are just part of our imperfect world. It's not so much the problems we have as how we deal with those problems. Many of us spend all of our time trying to figure out why we are suffering instead of figuring out what we can learn from the suffering. Just because we have problems doesn't mean that God is unhappy with us. If that were the case, he must have been really unhappy with Job, Wilford Woodruff, Spencer W. Kimball, and many others like them.

3. When suffering and opposition come into our lives, it is not a time to turn away from God, but rather to draw closer to him. God's redeeming grace is often felt the most in our hour of greatest need. One of the great blessings that comes to missionaries hundreds or even thousands of miles from home is not being able to call home. As they encounter homesickness, persecution, doubts, disappointments, and all types of opposition, they have only one place to turn— Heavenly Father. That loving Father becomes their source of strength and support.

What Opposition and Suffering Are

1. Opposition and suffering are a path to knowing God. One of the early pioneers in the Martin Handcart Company related:

"We suffered beyond anything you can imagine and many died of exposure and starvation, but did you ever hear a survivor of that company utter a word of criticism? Not one of that company ever apostatized or left the Church, because every one of us came through with the absolute knowledge that God lives, for we became acquainted with him in our extremities.

"I have pulled my handcart when I was so weak and weary from illness and lack of food that I could hardly put one foot ahead of the other. I have looked ahead and seen a patch of sand or a hill slope and I have said, I can go only that far and there I must give up, for I cannot pull the load through it. . . . I have looked back many times to see who was pushing my cart, but my eyes saw no one. I knew then that the angels of God were there.

"Was I sorry that I chose to come by handcart? No. Neither then nor any minute of my life since. The price we paid to become acquainted with God was a privilege to pay, and I am thankful that I was privileged to come in the Martin Handcart Company." (As quoted by David O. McKay, *Relief Society Magazine,* January 1948, p. 8.)

2. Opposition and suffering are God's way of sanctifying us. A few years ago, several large fires swept through Yellowstone Park in Wyoming. Our family was visiting the park at the time and could not believe the fires' destructive force. You can imagine our surprise when we heard an expert on a news report state that the fires might actually be good for the park. How could this be? The expert explained that the fires were burning all the old crowded brush. With all this old foliage gone, there would be room for newer and better growth. This experience brought to mind the fact that fire is not always destructive. Not only is it helpful in cleaning and renewing the growth of the forest, it is also the catalyst in refining metal. Those who produce metal use intense fire to burn off all the impurities.

Opposition and suffering are the fires that purify men's souls. In 1 Nephi we read, "For, behold, I have refined thee, I have chosen thee in the furnace of affliction" (1 Nephi 20:10). Commenting on this, Elder James E. Faust taught:

> Here then is a great truth. In the pain, the agony, and the heroic endeavors of life, we pass through a refiner's fire, and the insignificant and the unimportant in our lives can melt away like dross and make our faith bright, intact, and strong. In this way the divine image can be mirrored from the soul. It is part of the purging toll exacted of some to become acquainted with God. In the agonies of life, we seem to listen better to the faint, godly whisperings of the Divine Shepherd. (*Ensign,* May 1979, p. 53.)

3. Opposition and suffering are the means whereby we can understand and help others in their time of need. Many times after we have survived a trial in our life, others who are experiencing similar difficulties are led to us that we might give them comfort and help. Elder Orson F. Whitney described it this way:

> Men and women who have suffered, . . . bring forth the riches of their sympathy and condolences as a blessing to those now in need. Could they do this had they not suffered themselves?
> . . . Is not this God's purpose in causing his children to suffer? He wants them to become more like himself. God has suffered far more than man ever did or ever will, and is therefore the great source of sympathy and consolation. (*Improvement Era,* November 1918, p. 7.)

Jesus is able to give us such great comfort in part because of what he suffered. King Benjamin taught: "And lo, he shall suffer temptations, and pain of body, hunger, thirst, and fatigue, even more than man can suffer, except it be unto death; for behold, blood cometh from every pore, so great shall be his anguish for the wickedness and the abominations of his people" (Mosiah 3:7).

As opposition and suffering come to us, we can turn to the Savior knowing that he understands. In turn, we show our gratitude by offering counsel and comfort to others in need.

16

Happiness

What Happiness Is Not

1. **H**appiness is not something that can be acquired through worldly possessions, fame, wealth, or power. Happiness does not come from what we have but from what we are. Elder Richard G. Scott taught that "real joy comes from noble character, and that is built from a pattern of consistent, righteous decisions. Then the things we acquire are used as tools to help our own families and others." (*BYU 1988–89 Devotional and Fireside Speeches,* p. 135.)

Happiness isn't a new home, a new car, or a trip around the world. It isn't found in bank statements or stocks and bonds. Happiness comes from within and is enjoyed when our lives are right with God. This concept became very clear to a family that recently found themselves able to build a new home—one that they appreciated and loved. A short time later, their son was informed that the occupation he had desired and trained for would not be available to him. This occupation was something that their son had really set his heart on, and the news was a difficult and bitter pill for him to swallow. He would now have to spend another year in school and then spend a lifetime in a less-desired occupation. When he shared the news with his parents, they both realized that a new house meant nothing compared with the desires and needs of their family members.

Elder M. Russell Ballard had the opportunity of flying to Mexico with a television star and two very wealthy businessmen, one of whom was a billionaire. They flew in a private, executive jet owned by one of the men. Later Elder Ballard shared some of his feelings concerning this experience:

> By the time we landed at our destination, it had become abundantly clear to me that the billionaire, with all of his wealth, was really a most unhappy and spiritually deprived man. During the conversation I had learned that he had no children of his own. He had no definite faith in God and no positive assurance of hope for a life after death. . . .
>
> We completed our business in Mexico and again boarded the jet to return to Los Angeles. . . . When I walked into my home, my wife, Barbara, greeted me, and her first question to me was, "How did the meetings go?" My response to her question was, "Honey, we may not have very much money, but I do know this—of the four men aboard that plane, I was by far the richest man of them all because I was the only one who knew where I came from, why I am here on this earth, and where I can go in the eternities to come if I am faithful."
>
> My wife and I discussed this experience, and as we did, again the words of the Lord seemed to ring clearly in my mind, [He that hath eternal life is rich]. (*New Era,* December 1977, pp. 5–6.)

2. "Wickedness never was happiness" (Alma 41:10). Samuel, the great Lamanite prophet, taught this: "Ye have sought for happiness in doing iniquity, which thing is contrary to the nature of that righteousness which is in our great and Eternal Head" (Helaman 13:38).

President Ezra Taft Benson made this fundamental concept very clear when he warned, "*Wickedness never did, never does, never will* bring us happiness. Violation of the laws of God brings only misery, bondage, and darkness." (*Ensign,* October 1989, p. 2.)

Drinking, pornography, smutty movies and television shows, vulgar jokes, and immorality are all participated in by those seeking happiness. These people have been misled, and, instead of happiness, they receive only inferior sensations of pleasure—many of which leave guilt, distress, unhappiness, distrust, and a loss of the Spirit.

3. Happiness is not the same as pleasure. Referring to Lehi's vision of the tree of life, Elder Glenn L. Pace discussed the difference between happiness and pleasure:

> Even though you have a testimony and want to do what is right, it is difficult not to be drawn to the great and spacious building. From all appearances, the people in the building seem to be having a great time. The music and laughter are deafening. You would say to me what my children have said, "They're not really happy, huh, Dad?" as you watch them party.
>
> They look happy and free, but don't mistake telestial pleasure for celestial happiness and joy. Don't mistake lack of self-control for freedom. . . . Don't envy a lesser and lower life. (*Ensign,* November 1987, p. 40.)

Pleasure is temporary; happiness is long lasting. Happiness is accompanied by peace; many times, pleasure brings guilt, remorse, and degradation. True happiness is lived over and over again in our memories; pleasure is transitory. Elder James E. Talmage described happiness well when he wrote: "Happiness is not akin with levity, nor is it one with light-minded mirth. It springs from the deeper fountains of the soul, and is infrequently accompanied by tears." (*Improvement Era,* December 1913, p. 173.)

What Happiness Is

1. Happiness is a by-product of sincere Christian service. This was forever learned by one Laurel class. Shortly before Christmas, these young women arranged to bring joy to a lonely widow named Jane. They baked cookies, planned special refreshments, wrapped gifts, purchased a beautiful corsage, and obtained a Christmas tree and ornaments to decorate the tree.

They erected the Christmas tree in Jane's apartment and enthusiastically covered it with the beautiful decorations they had so carefully brought. Brightly covered packages were placed under the tree, and the refreshments were prepared and enjoyed.

Jane then gathered the girls around her and shared with them some of her most precious memories. They learned of her conversion in Scotland and of the abuse she suffered in order to adhere to the teachings of the gospel. She told them of her storm-filled voyage to America and the warm feeling she felt when she saw the Statue of Liberty. As the girls listened, their hearts were touched and their eyes filled with tears. As they felt Jane's sweet spirit of faith and commitment, they found themselves quietly pledging to live the gospel and keep the Lord's standards in their own lives. President Thomas S. Monson described the impact this evening of service had upon Jane and upon the girls who were willing to share:

> As the evening came to an end, there were kisses and embraces; and then each young lady filed silently from the doorway and made her way down the staircases to the street outside. They left behind a mother filled with the goodness of the world, with love rekindled, with faith again inspired. I'm certain this was one of the happiest days of her life. That night the corsage was carefully and tenderly placed in safekeeping. It had become a symbol of all that is good and clean and wholesome.
>
> Outside the snow was falling, and the girls could hear the crunch of their own footsteps on the snow-covered pavement. Words didn't come easily, and then one Laurel girl asked, "Why is it I feel better than I've ever felt before?" Others nodded the same curiosity. I answered them, "Remember the words of the Master: 'Inasmuch as ye have done it unto one of the least of these . . . , ye have done it unto me.'" (Matt. 25:40.) (*Ensign,* November 1990, p. 99.)

2. Happiness comes through gospel living. The purpose of our lives here is to obtain a fulness of joy through obedience to God's commandments. After a family had read 2 Nephi 2:25, which states that "Adam fell that men might be; and men are, that they might have joy," the father asked his eight-year-old daughter what she thought this scripture meant. She responded, " 'I'm not sure about the first

part, . . . but the last part means we're supposed to be happy.' " (R. Val Johnson, *Ensign,* April 1993, p. 22.) This scripture has never been explained better than it was by this insightful eight-year-old, for God's overwhelming desire for us is that we share in the happiness that he enjoys. The Prophet Joseph Smith taught that God "never will institute an ordinance or give a commandment to His people that is not calculated in its nature to promote that happiness which He has designed" (*History of the Church,* 5:135).

The soul-deep happiness that accompanies gospel obedience has little to do with pleasure and comes when our lives are in harmony with the Spirit and the will of God. This happiness takes consistent effort and serious commitment, but, as Lehi testified, the result is well worth the struggle. After seeing a vision of the tree of life, Lehi described the joy that came from partaking of its fruit: "As I partook of the fruit thereof it filled my soul with exceedingly great joy: wherefore, I began to be desirous that my family should partake of it also; for I knew that it was desirable above all other fruit" (1 Nephi 8:12).

3. The happiness that comes from gospel living is eternal. The world's pleasures are temporary and unpredictable, as expressed by a young girl who had spent the afternoon enjoying a picnic with a friend. The day had been a beautiful one, and her friend had said to her, "Don't you just feel happy inside?"

This ten- or eleven-year-old girl surprised her friend when she answered, "No, I don't."

When her friend asked her why she didn't feel happy, she said, "Because it won't last. You can be happy for a minute, but not for very long. Life just doesn't make sense to me." (Michaelene P. Grassli, *Ensign,* November 1988, p. 90.)

No one had taught this girl about a happiness that can last through good times and bad times and continue on into eternity. God's happiness is consistent and enduring, and a deep and lasting joy is awaiting those who take advantage of his magnificent plan. The better we live the plan, the more peace and joy we receive until, eventually in the celestial kingdom, a fulness of joy will be ours. God has given his solemn word that this is true, and God does not vary "from that which he hath said" (D&C 3:2).

17

Service

What Service Is Not

1. Service is not conditional. One of Satan's deceptive tools is to create counterfeits to the Lord's way of doing things. We must be careful that we understand the difference between the kind of service the Lord teaches and the false service that Satan teaches. Satan's service disguises selfishness under the cloak of service. For example, some serve with strings attached or because certain service is personally advantageous. Some are offended if their service is not appreciated. Others serve only those they feel are worthy of such service or serve only out of obligation. All of these kinds of service are conditional. The true blessings of service never accompany such feelings and behavior.

On the other hand, service the Lord's way is given unconditionally. Elder H. Burke Peterson explained the difference:

A selfless person is one who is more concerned about the happiness and well-being of another than about his or her own convenience or comfort, one who is willing to serve another when it is neither sought for nor appreciated, or one who is willing to serve even those whom he or she dislikes. A selfless person displays a willingness to sacrifice, a willingness to purge from his or her mind and heart personal wants, and needs, and feelings. Instead of reaching for and requiring praise and recognition for himself, or gratification of his or her own wants, the selfless person will meet these very human needs for others. (*Ensign,* May 1985, p. 66.)

2. Great service is not always something big. Some of the greatest acts ever performed are the small and simple ones. It is the little daily acts of service that make the difference in people's lives. The Savior put it this way: "Wherefore, be not weary in well-doing, for ye are laying the foundation of a great work. And out of small things proceedeth that which is great." (D&C 64:33.)

President Spencer W. Kimball taught:

God does notice us, and he watches over us. But it is usually through another mortal that he meets our needs. Therefore, it is vital that we serve each other in the kingdom. . . .

So often, our acts of service consist of simple encouragement or of giving mundane help with mundane tasks—but what glorious consequences can flow from mundane acts and from small but deliberate deeds! (*The Teachings of Spencer W. Kimball,* p. 252.)

3. Service is not always giving. For many of us it is easier to give than to receive. However, some of the greatest acts of service we will ever render will be the humble acceptance of service from someone else. All of us need to learn to accept service from others. When we graciously receive these acts of service, we are also serving those who serve us. By letting others do things for us, we build a bond of friendship and love, which is one of the greatest gifts that we could ever give.

Many have learned the great blessings that can come to those who are on the receiving end of service. Brenda was a very capable woman who had spent her life giving service to others. Only when she was stricken with a disabling illness did she learn the blessings that come to those who receive service. At first, as friends and neighbors came to her home to help clean the house and care for her family, she felt very uncomfortable and wished they weren't there. But as time wore on, she found her resentment and guilt changing to love. She developed a bond of love for those people that grew in a way she had never dreamed possible. In return, those who rendered the service found themselves loving Brenda and her family more deeply than ever before.

What Service Is

1. Service is a privilege. Real service is not something we have to do, but rather something we get to do. Our attitude is as important as the service: how we think of the service we give will directly influence the quality of our actions. Moroni understood well, for he taught:

> For behold, God hath said a man being evil cannot do that which is good; for if he offereth a gift, or prayeth unto God, except he shall do it with real intent it profiteth him nothing.
> For behold, it is not counted unto him for righteousness.
> For behold, if a man being evil giveth a gift, he doeth it grudgingly; wherefore it is counted unto him the same as if he had retained the gift; wherefore he is counted evil before God. (Moroni 7:6–8.)

To illustrate this principle, let us consider home teaching and visiting teaching. Some view these calls as something that has to be done out of duty or obligation. Others, however, see it as an opportunity to serve. To them it is a privilege and honor to represent our Father in Heaven and his Son. These two attitudes offer a wide variation in the type of teaching and visiting that will be done.

A good example of this is a man who was assigned as a home teacher to a dear sister who had been incapacitated for eight years. She was unable to walk or talk and was confined to a bed. He assessed the couple's real needs and could see that caring for this sister totally encompassed every moment of her good husband's life. The home teacher asked if his wife could come over to the house every Sunday morning and stay with the invalid woman while her husband attended priesthood meeting. For six years, every Sunday this home teacher would bring his wife over to stay with the invalid sister while her husband went to his meeting. And every Sunday the home teacher's wife would bring with her some baked goods or something special that she had made for this older couple.

Eventually the sister who was ill passed away. When her daughter tried to express her deep love and appreciation to the home teacher and his wife for what they had done over the years, the wife said, "Oh, don't thank us. It was our privilege to visit with your sweet mother. What am I going to do now? The hour and a half on Sunday morning will now be, for me, the loneliest hour and a half in the week." (See J. Richard Clarke, *Ensign,* November 1981, p. 81.)

2. Service is a good way to solve personal problems. When we serve others, not only do we help others but we are also able to see our own problems more clearly. President Spencer W. Kimball taught that only by serving do we learn how to serve: "In the midst of the miracle of serving, there is the promise of Jesus, that by losing ourselves, we find ourselves. Not only do we 'find' ourselves in terms of acknowledging guidance in our lives, but the more we serve our fellowmen in appropriate ways, the more substance there is to our souls." (*The Teachings of Spencer W. Kimball,* p. 254.) President Ezra Taft Benson taught:

> To lose yourself in righteous service to others can lift your sights and get your mind off personal problems, or at least put them in proper focus. "When you find yourselves a little gloomy," said President Lorenzo Snow, "look around you and find somebody that is in a worse plight than yourself; go to him and find out what the trouble is, then try to remove it with the wisdom which the Lord bestows upon you; and the first thing you know, your gloom is gone, you feel light, the Spirit of the Lord is upon you, and everything seems illuminated. (Conference Report, 6 April 1899, pp. 2–3.)" (Conference Report, October 1974, p. 91.)

3. Service is an eternal investment. The things of this world will rot and waste away, but the children of God are eternal. The time spent

serving mankind will bring not only immediate blessings but also eternal joy in the world to come. The greatest service and most eternal investment of all is sharing the truths of the gospel with our brothers and sisters. The Lord made this clear when he said:

Remember the worth of souls is great in the sight of God; . . .

And if it so be that you should labor all your days in crying repentance unto this people, and bring, save it be one soul unto me, how great shall be your joy with him in the kingdom of my Father!

And now, if your joy will be great with one soul that you have brought unto me into the kingdom of my Father, how great will be your joy if you should bring many souls unto me! (D&C 18:10, 15–16.)

As we lovingly serve others and God, we come to know the Savior better and become more like him. King Benjamin emphasized this important truth when he stated, "For how knoweth a man the master whom he has not served" (Mosiah 5:13).

18

Foreordination

Because it can be so easily misunderstood, foreordination is often a difficult doctrine to discuss. In fact, it is one of the least understood doctrines of the Church. Discussing the challenge of teaching foreordination, Elder Neal A. Maxwell said:

> The doctrine of foreordination is one of the doctrinal roads "least traveled by." . . . It is so powerful a doctrine, however, that, isolated from other doctrines, or mishandled, it can stoke the fires of fatalism, impact adversely upon agency, cause us to focus on status rather than service, and carry us over into predestination. (District sacrament meeting in Jerusalem, October 1978.)

Discussing foreordination without making some reference to the complex doctrines of agency and the foreknowledge of God is both difficult and dangerous. Since God has not revealed the answers to many of our questions concerning foreordination, we must simply accept some things on faith.

The inherent doctrinal hazards associated with foreordination make it especially important to emphasize some of the things that foreordination is not. This will greatly facilitate our comprehension of what it is and why it is so important.

What Foreordination Is Not

1. Foreordination is not predestination. Although the King James translators used the term *predestination* in Paul's writings, President Joseph Fielding Smith warned:

> Surely Paul never intended to convey such a thought. . . . This might have been one of the passages in Paul's teachings which caused Peter to declare that there are in Paul's writings, "some things hard to be understood, which they that are unlearned and unstable, wrest as they do also the other scriptures, unto their own destruction." (*Improvement Era,* May 1963, pp. 350–51.)

Those who are foreordained are not guaranteed blessings but are given special opportunities to serve. If they fulfill these responsibilities then promised blessings will come into their lives.

2. Foreordination does not guarantee success. Some feel that those who have been foreordained cannot fail in what they have been chosen to do. This simply is not true. Samson was foreordained to do great things and was born with tremendous promise and potential, but the scriptures clearly reveal that he used the strength God had given him for his own self-indulgence and failed to live up to his calling and covenants. Elder Harold B. Lee taught that those things we have been foreordained to do will come to pass only if we are faithful and obedient:

> I fear there are many among us who because of their faithfulness in the spirit world were "called" to do a great work here, but like reckless spend thrifts they are exercising their free agency in riotous living and are losing their birthright and the blessings that were theirs had they proved faithful to their calling. Hence as the Lord has said, "There are many called but few are chosen." (*Youth and the Church,* p. 169.)

3. There is no compulsion or force involved in foreordination. Although foreordination is closely associated with God's foreknowl-

edge, our not knowing what is to come preserves our free agency completely. Elder James E. Talmage explained:

> Many people have been led to regard this foreknowledge of God as a predestination whereby souls are designated for glory or condemnation even before their birth in the flesh. . . . How dreadful, how inconsistent is such an idea of God! It leads to the absurd conclusion that the mere knowledge of coming events must act as a determining influence in bringing about these occurrences. God's knowledge of spiritual and of human nature enables Him to conclude with certainty as to the actions of any of His children under given conditions; yet that knowledge is not of compelling force upon the creature. (*Articles of Faith*, p. 191.)

What Foreordination Is

Foreordination is similar to several earthly blessings that we receive, such as patriarchal blessings, ordinations, setting apart blessings, and the special blessing we receive when we are given a name shortly after entering this world. The Lord charges us to do certain things and promises his great power and direction if we accept and fulfill the charge. Just as we are ordained or set apart to certain callings and positions here, we were foreordained in premortality to certain roles or responsibilities in the kingdom of God. Joseph Smith taught that "every man who has a calling to minister to the inhabitants of the world was ordained to that very purpose in the grand council of heaven before this world was" (*History of the Church*, 6:364).

When we are ordained or set apart to an office or calling, men lay their hands upon our heads and through inspiration pronounce upon us certain powers and instructions pertaining to our specific calling. Is it too much to assume that foreordinations were performed the same way—that those with authority in heaven (possibly even our Father or the Savior in many instances) laid their hands upon our heads and lovingly bestowed upon us responsibilities and blessings pertaining to this life? Elder Bruce R. McConkie explained: "In all this there is not the slightest hint of compulsion. . . . By their foreordination the Lord merely gives them the opportunity to serve him and his purposes if they will choose to measure up to the standard he knows they are capable of attaining." (*Mormon Doctrine,* p. 290.)

Our Heavenly Father has a full knowledge and understanding of our strengths and weaknesses. Our individual foreordinations are linked to our past performances and to our specific talents, attitudes, and abilities. God would never foreordain us to do something that is beyond our capacity to do but will, if we are willing, "prepare a way for [us] that [we] may accomplish the thing which he" has foreordained us to do (see 1 Nephi 3:7).

We do not need to know what our specific foreordination is in order to fulfill our special pre-earth assignments. As we place God first in our lives and serve him with all our might, mind, and strength, the Spirit will direct us and we will automatically and naturally accomplish those responsibilities we have been called and foreordained to do.

19

The Sacrament

What the Sacrament Is Not

1. The sacrament is not optional. If we are to properly keep our covenants of baptism we must partake of the sacrament regularly. When it comes to renewing and keeping our baptismal covenants, the sacrament is the vital link between us and our Heavenly Father. If we fail to partake of the sacrament, his Spirit will eventually leave us and we will be left to ourselves and Satan's influence. President Joseph Fielding Smith taught:

> No member of the Church can fail to make this covenant [the sacrament] and renew it week by week, and retain the Spirit of the Lord. The Sacrament meeting of the Church is the most important meeting which we have, and is sadly neglected by many members. We go to this service, if we understand the purpose of it, not primarily to hear someone speak, important though that may be, but first, and most important, to renew this covenant with our Father in heaven in the name of Jesus Christ. Those who persist in their absence from this service will eventually lose the Spirit, and if

they do not repent will eventually find themselves denying the faith. (*Church History and Modern Revelation,* 1:132.)

The sacrament's importance in our spiritual well-being was demonstrated in the lives of a couple whose son was preparing to be married in the temple. The couple went to their bishop to get a temple recommend so they could attend their son's wedding. During the interview the mother admitted that she was drinking coffee daily. The bishop said he could not issue her a recommend until she stopped drinking coffee. He challenged her to stop and promised that the Lord would help her. He pointed out to her that she had plenty of time to stop before the wedding.

Instead of stopping the habit, she left the bishop's office in a huff, saying that she would never come back to church as long as he was the bishop. She kept her promise and missed her son's wedding. As the years passed and several bishops were sustained and released, she never came back. Instead, she lost the Spirit and denied the faith.

This sad story does not end there. Her failure to partake of the sacrament and retain the Spirit not only led her from the great blessings she could have had but also adversely affected most of her children, who have also lost the Spirit and denounced the Church.

This example serves as a strong reminder to us that the sacrament is not something that can be taken lightly or neglected. Our worthy participation in this sacred ordinance is essential to our eternal happiness and progression.

2. The sacrament is not a time to mentally and spiritually wander. One of the sacrament's major purposes is to provide a time each week for us to remember and renew our covenants with Heavenly Father. However, far too often we let the things of the world distract us. While the sacrament is being passed, our minds wander home to dinner or to the next row to check on a conversation that is taking place. We cannot allow such distractions to clutter our minds and deny us the real blessings of the sacrament.

While the sacrament is being administered, we need to focus our attention on the meaning and purpose of the sacrament. There are several ways to do this. One is to listen carefully to the sacramental prayers and then read or recite the prayers to ourselves while the sacrament is being passed, focusing on the three promises we make when we partake of the sacrament. Elder David O. McKay explained those three promises as follows:

> The first: That we are willing to take upon ourselves the name of the Son. In so doing we choose him as our leader and our ideal; and he is the one perfect character in all the world. It is a glorious thing to be a member of the Church of Christ and to be called a Christian in the true sense of the term; and we promise that we should like to be that, that we are willing to do it.
>
> Secondly, that we will always remember him. Not just on Sunday, but on Monday, in our daily acts, in our self-control. When our brother hurts us are we going to try to master our feelings and not retaliate in the same spirit of anger? When a brother treats us with contempt, are we going to try to return kindness? That's the spirit of the Christ and that's what we have promised— that we will do our best to achieve these high stands of Christianity, true Christian principles.
>
> The third: We promise to "keep the commandments which he has given." Tithing, fast offerings, the Word of Wisdom, kindness, forgiveness, love. The obligation of a member of the Church of Christ is great, but it is as glorious as it is great, because obedience to these principles gives life eternal. On the other hand, the man who seeks to live by violating the principles is deceived by the adversary and goes the way to death. (Conference Report, October 1929, p. 14.)

Another way of focusing our attention is to mentally review the Savior's sacred mission and all he did for us. "It is said of President Wilford Woodruff that while the sacrament was being passed, his lips could be observed in silent motion as he repeated to himself over and over again, 'I do remember thee, I do remember thee' " (Marion G. Romney, *Ensign,* October 1976, p. 3).

A third way is to silently review our actions of the past week and look toward the week to come. As we examine the past week, we need to "check in" with our Father in Heaven on how we did with our commitments of that week. Then we need to resolve certain decisions for the week to come. A silent prayer to Heavenly Father expressing gratitude, repentance, and commitment is very appropriate and helpful during the sacrament. Elder Howard W. Hunter stated: "The solemn moments of thought while the sacrament is being served have great significance. They are moments of self-examination, introspection, self-discernment—a time to reflect and to resolve." (*Ensign,* May 1977, p. 25.)

What the Sacrament Is

1. The sacrament can give us hope and strength. There is a sacred power that always comes through worthily partaking of the sacrament—a power that is not fully understood by mankind. However, this we do know: the sacrament prayer renews the promise that we will always have his Spirit with us. As we worthily partake of the sacrament, we welcome the Holy Ghost into our lives, and it is the Holy Ghost who gives us hope and strength beyond our natural ability. Elder John H. Groberg observed, "As we worthily partake of the sacrament we will sense those things we need to improve in and receive the help and determination to do so. No matter what our problems, the sacrament always gives hope." (*Ensign,* May 1989, p. 38.)

2. The sacrament is food for the spirit. We all enter sacrament meeting with various spiritual hungers. The Lord is prepared to feed us if we allow him to do so. He knows what we need and how best to satisfy our hungry souls. All we must do is seek his help as we partake of the sacrament. Elder Melvin J. Ballard taught:

> How can we have spiritual hunger? Who is there among us that does not wound his spirit by word, thought, or deed, from Sabbath to Sabbath? We do things for which we are sorry and desire to be forgiven, or we have erred against someone and given injury. If there is a feeling in our hearts that we are sorry for what we have done; if there is a feeling in our souls that we would like to be forgiven, then the method to obtain forgiveness is not through rebaptism . . . but it is to repent of our sins, to go to those against whom we have sinned or transgressed and obtain their forgiveness, and

then repair to the sacrament table, where, if we have sincerely repented and put ourselves in proper condition, we shall be forgiven, and spiritual healing will come to our souls. (*Improvement Era,* October 1919, p. 1026.)

3. The sacrament is a reminder of our covenants. As we come to understand the great power the sacrament can have in our lives, we realize that it serves as a reminder of the covenants we have made with Heavenly Father. As we keep those covenants we find that we are protected against apostasy, which is brought about by the fiery darts of Satan. President Spencer W. Kimball explained:

> That is the real purpose of the sacrament, to keep us from forgetting, to help us to remember. I suppose there would never be an apostate, there would never be a crime, if people remembered, really remembered, the things they had covenanted at the water's edge or at the sacrament table and in the temple. I suppose that is the reason the Lord asked Adam to offer sacrifices, for no other reason than that he and his posterity would remember—remember the basic things that they had been taught. I guess we as humans are prone to forget. It is easy to forget. Our sorrows, our joys, our concerns, our great problems seem to wane to some extent as time goes on, and there are many lessons that we learn which have a tendency to slip from us. The Nephites forgot. They forgot the days when they felt good.
>
> I remember a young Navaho boy returning from his mission who was supported largely by a seventies quorum in the Bonneville Stake. I happened to be present the day he made his report and as tears rolled down his face, he said, "Oh, if I could only remember always just how I feel now." (*The Teachings of Spencer W. Kimball,* p. 112.)

20

Eternal Marriage

What Eternal Marriage Is Not

1. Eternal marriage is not optional for exaltation in the celestial kingdom. Those who live celestial lives and are not married for eternity may go to the celestial kingdom, but they cannot be exalted (become gods and goddesses and have spirit children of their own). This vital gospel principle is clearly taught in D&C 131:1–4:

> In the celestial glory there are three heavens or degrees;
> And in order to obtain the highest, a man must enter into this order of the priesthood [meaning the new and everlasting covenant of marriage];
> And if he does not, he cannot obtain it.
> He may enter into the other, but that is the end of his kingdom; he cannot have an increase.

To not "have an increase" means that we cannot have spirit children of our own. This makes sense because we cannot have children if we do not have a husband or a wife. Without the ability to procreate spirit children of our own to place on earths and help grow toward godhood, we cannot become gods; therefore, we would become ministering angels to work with the spirit children of those who have become gods. The critical importance of eternal marriage in our quest for exaltation was emphasized by President Spencer W. Kimball when he wrote:

> Any of you would go around the world for the sealing ordinance if you knew its importance, if you realized how great it is. No distance, no shortage of funds, no situation would ever keep you from being married in the holy temple of the Lord.
>
> There is no bias nor prejudice in this doctrine. It is a matter of following a certain program to reach a definite goal. If you fail in following a program, you fail in attaining the goal. . . .
>
> . . . No one who rejects the covenant of celestial marriage can reach exaltation in the eternal kingdom of God. . . .
>
> Some might say, "Well, I'd be satisfied to just become an angel," but you would not. One never would be satisfied just to be a ministering angel to wait upon other people when he could be the king himself. (*Ensign,* October 1979, pp. 4–6.)

2. A marriage is not eternal just because it was performed in a holy temple. John K. Edmunds, who was the president of the Salt Lake Temple for many years, performed hundreds of temple sealings. At many of these marriages, he gave the bride and groom the following counsel:

> We can give you the ordinance, but we can't give you eternal marriage. That is your decision; that is your job. That you must earn. You must endure in righteousness to the end. You have nothing made by simply coming here. Nothing is ever made that you do not make yourself. You will have to continue in righteousness, to the end of your lives, living "by every word that proceedeth forth from the mouth of God." (D&C 84:44.) (*Ensign,* July 1976, p. 69.)

Some people have lied to priesthood leaders in order to participate in the temple. Others have not continued to keep the commandments after partaking of the sealing ordinance. Some of these people mistakenly believe that they have an eternal marriage. There is an enormous difference between being married in the temple and having an eternal or celestial marriage. The first is an event, the second a process that takes a lifetime. President Spencer W. Kimball described the process of obtaining an eternal marriage when he declared:

> First, there must be the proper approach toward marriage, which contemplates the selection of a spouse who reaches as nearly as possible the pinnacle of perfection in all the matters which are of importance to the individuals. And then those two parties must come to the altar in the temple realizing that they must work hard toward this successful joint living.
>
> Second, there must be a great unselfishness, forgetting self and directing all of the family life and all pertaining thereunto to the good of the family, subjugating self.
>
> Third, there must be continued courting and expressions of affection, kindness, and consideration to keep love alive and growing.
>
> Fourth, there must be a complete living of the commandments of the Lord as defined in the gospel of Jesus Christ. (*The Teachings of Spencer W. Kimball,* p. 306.)

As we live the gospel and keep the covenants that we have made with our Father in Heaven, the Holy Ghost is able to seal our ordinances, including our temple sealing, and they become binding for eternity (see D&C 132:7). Our righteousness and obedience are essential ingredients in making our temple wedding an eternal marriage.

3. Eternal marriage is not something to be entered into lightly. President Spencer W. Kimball taught that before we were ever born we made solemn vows with our Heavenly Father that "we would keep our lives clean and would marry in the holy temple and would rear a family and teach them righteousness. This was a solemn oath, a solemn promise." (Quoted by Barbara W. Winder, *BYU 1989–90 Devotional and Fireside Speeches,* p. 195.)

When we kneel with our chosen companion at the altar in the temple, we renew these sacred vows and promise again that we will obey God and keep his commandments. Great blessings come through covenant making and obedience, but it is better to not make a covenant than to make one and not strive to keep it. The Lord explained this to some Saints when he said:

> And as the covenant which they made unto me has been broken, even so it has become void and of none effect.
>
> And wo to him by whom this offense cometh, for it had been better for him that he had been drowned in the depth of the sea.
>
> But blessed are they who have kept the covenant and observed the commandment, for they shall obtain mercy. (D&C 54:4–6.)

The Lord has told us that where "much is given much is required" and that those who sin "against the greater light shall receive the greater condemnation" (D&C 82:3). The endowment and sealing covenants offer marvelous blessings, but they must be entered into soberly and seriously. The Lord expects us to do our very best to keep our part of the agreement.

What Eternal Marriage Is

1. Eternal marriage is something we need to take advantage of *now!* President Kimball told of a good man who passed away. He and his wife had ignored the teachings of the Church and had not partaken of the eternal sealing ordinances performed in the temple. After his death his wife said, "I know that we will be associated as husband and wife through eternity."

President Kimball's response to this statement was very clear: "She could say that a thousand times and it would still not come true because they were not humble enough to accept the law of marriage. They may receive other blessings, but not exaltation. That is reserved for those who are faithful and who obey the commandments." (*The Teachings of Spencer W. Kimball*, p. 298.)

Many couples talk about going to the temple someday. Others have been to the temple but are not now living the gospel in such a way that their temple ordinances are valid. Some of these couples may even be using the word *soon* to describe when they will decide to repent and become obedient or partake of the temple blessings for the first time. Soon is not soon enough. Death or other problems can come unexpectedly and blessings can be forever lost. The Lord has promised us that they who seek him "*early* shall find rest to their souls" (D&C 54:10; italics added). Exaltation is just too important for us to put it off. Now is the time to begin ensuring our eternal future.

2. Eternal marriage is promised to those who faithfully keep the commandments but do not have this opportunity during this life. To these people, President Kimball made the following promise:

> We promise you that insofar as eternity is concerned, no soul will be deprived of rich and high and eternal blessings for anything which that person could not help, that the Lord never fails in his promises, and that every righteous person will receive eventually all to which the person is entitled and which he or she has not forfeited through any fault of his or her own. We encourage both men and women to keep themselves well-groomed, well-dressed, abreast of the times, attractive mentally, spiritually, physically, and especially morally, and then they can lean heavily upon the Lord's promises for these heavenly blessings. (*Ensign,* October 1979, p. 5.)

3. Who and where we marry is the most important decision we ever make. Elder Bruce R. McConkie wrote that "the most important single thing that any Latter-day Saint ever does in this world is to marry the *right* person in the *right* place by the *right* authority" (*Choose an Eternal Companion,* p. 2).

In spite of the eternal significance of marriage, some people seem to spend more time planning the honeymoon than considering their marriage decision. One couple met in a park, talked for a few minutes, went to the courthouse, were married, returned to the park for a hot dog, talked a few more minutes, found they had nothing in common, and decided to separate.

In one of the western states, a law was passed that established a twenty-four-hour waiting period between obtaining the marriage certificate and being married. One third of the couples changed their minds during that waiting period and decided not to marry. It is apparent that they had not thought sufficiently about their marriage decision.

This most important of all decisions should be approached with much fasting and prayer and with a sincere desire to gain the Lord's will on the matter. We know that he wants us to marry in the temple, but we need his guidance in order to make sure that we marry the right person at the right time.

21

Personal Revelation

What Personal Revelation Is Not

1. **P**ersonal revelation is not always from God. Doug and Mary had been married six years, in which time they had accumulated substantial debt. One of their three small children had been the source of some enormous medical bills. Doug felt he needed to get some schooling so he could upgrade his employment situation. He was working two jobs trying to make ends meet. Both Doug and Mary were hoping and praying for some way that they could solve their financial dilemma.

One of Doug's jobs was working for a company that constructed prebuilt homes. He worked as a supervisor of the night shift. For several weeks Doug noticed that after each home was completed, some perfectly good materials were left over. Their need for extra money and the apparent excess of materials made him think about how the two problems could be solved at the same time. He decided that he could sell the excess materials to other contractors. It seemed to him that this could be a possible answer to their prayers concerning their financial problems. He could see the potential of paying off their debt in a short period of time and putting away enough money to finance his education. As he talked the idea over with Mary, she became excited at the prospect of ridding themselves of debt and completing Doug's education. They decided that Doug would contact various contractors and sell them the materials at a reduced price. He would remove the materials from the plant when it was vacant at the end of the night shift. Because Doug was left alone to close up, he could have the contractors come to the plant in the early hours of the morning before the day crew arrived. Everything seemed to be falling into place except for one problem. Doug and Mary had spent a great deal of time discussing the merits of whether it was an honest thing to do. They finally decided that it was probably not honest or legal, but it seemed like an answer to their prayers. They became confused and decided to ask the Lord if it was honest. As they prayed, they felt the Lord was telling them to go ahead with their plans to sell the materials. So they proceeded.

Everything went smoothly for about two months—until a police car showed up one morning as Doug was loading materials into one of his buyer's trucks. He was arrested, charged with theft, and later convicted. He was required to repay the cost of the materials and spend time in jail. As you can imagine, things for Doug and Mary went from bad to worse. In their confusion, they questioned why Doug had been arrested when they had received personal revelation that this was the right thing to do.

The answer to this couple's question is simple. They received their personal revelation from the wrong source. The Lord will never tell us to do things that are wrong. He has made it clear that we should be honest in all that we do. Their first mistake was asking the Lord to give them an answer to something that he had already answered. When we do this, we open ourselves up to receiving answers from Satan. Elder Boyd K. Packer commented on this:

> All inspiration does not come from God. (See D&C 46:7.) The evil one has the power to tap into those channels of revelation and send conflicting signals which can mislead and confuse us. There are promptings from evil sources which are so carefully counterfeited as to deceive even the very elect. (See Matt. 24:24.)
>
> Nevertheless, we can learn to discern these spirits. Even with every member having the right to revelation, the Church can be maintained as a house of order. (*Ensign,* November 1989, p. 14.)

The question then arises—how do we avoid being deceived? One suggestion is to avoid praying about whether something is right when we already know the answer. Some things are very clear. For example, the Lord has made it clear that we should be faithful to our spouse. To ask the Lord if it is all right to become involved romantically with someone else while we are married is setting ourselves up to get personal revelation from the wrong source.

Another suggestion is to work at finding the answer before going to the Lord (see D&C 9:7–9). In Doug and Mary's case, they could have asked the owner of the plant what he thought about the idea and obtained his permission. They also could have talked to their priesthood leaders and studied the scriptures and words of the living prophets on the subject.

Elder Bruce R. McConkie gave us another simple suggestion on how to get personal revelation from God:

1. Search the scriptures.

2. Keep the commandments.

3. Ask in faith. (See *How to Get Personal Revelation,* p. 8.)

2. Personal revelation is not for others. The word *personal* is the key. It means just that. When the Lord reveals something concerning our personal lives, he intends it only for us. Too many times we want to transfer our revelation to others' lives. Concerning the proper use of personal revelation, Elder Boyd K. Packer taught:

> An unusual spiritual experience should not be regarded as a personal call to direct others. It is my conviction that experiences of a special, sacred nature are individual and should be kept to oneself.
>
> Few things disturb the channels of revelation quite so effectively as those who are misled and think themselves to be chosen to instruct others when they are not chosen. (*Ensign,* November 1989, p. 15.)

The only exception to this is when we have been given a stewardship by the Lord, such as a calling in the Church or that of being a parent. But even at that we need to be careful that we stay within the proper bounds of our calling. When we step outside those bounds we open ourselves up to be deceived. Lindsay R. Curtis declared:

The keystone to our Church is revelation. Beginning with revelation through our prophets for the Church as a whole, it continues through the General Authorities, each in his specific calling, and through the various other authorities—regional representatives, stake presidents, bishops, organizational heads, quorum presidents, home teachers, heads of families, and individuals. Each of these is entitled to revelation concerning his own responsibility. (*New Era,* March 1984, p. 13.)

Elder Boyd K. Packer further instructed us on this matter when he said:

Revelation comes in an orderly way in the Church. We are entitled to personal revelation. However, unless we are set apart to some presiding office, we will not receive revelations concerning what others should do.

Revelation in the Church comes to those who have been properly called, sustained, ordained, or set apart. A bishop, for instance, will not receive any revelation concerning a neighboring ward, because that is out of his jurisdiction. (*Ensign,* November 1989, pp. 14–15.)

What Personal Revelation Is

1. Personal revelation is a privilege and obligation that all may receive. When we make the decision to commit our life to the Savior through the ordinance of baptism, we receive the gift of the Holy Ghost. This wonderful gift is a promise that we may have the constant companionship of the Holy Ghost as long as we live worthy of it. The Holy Ghost is the channel through which the Lord gives us personal revelation. Therefore, as a member of the Savior's church, one of the promises and blessings we receive is the privilege to receive personal revelation. President Wilford Woodruff taught concerning this privilege:

Every man or woman that has ever entered into the church of God and been baptized for the remission of sins has a right to revelation, a right to the Spirit of God, to assist them in their labors, in their administrations to their children, . . . and those over whom they are called upon to preside (*Millennial Star,* 51:548).

As members of the Church, we have not only the privilege of receiving personal revelation but also the obligation to do so. Each member has the obligation to learn through personal revelation that the Church's principles and practices are true. More important, however, they have the responsibility to receive a personal witness that Jesus is the Christ.

2. Personal revelation is the foundation upon which our salvation is built. It is well understood that the foundation of any building keeps it upright. When that foundation is weak or destroyed, the rest of the building is affected likewise. So it is with our salvation. The foundation of our salvation is based on our individual knowledge received through personal revelation of the Savior and his mission. Joseph Smith understood this when he said: "Salvation cannot come without revelation; it is in vain for anyone to minister it. No man is a minister of Jesus Christ without being a Prophet. No man can be a minister of Jesus Christ except he has the testimony of Jesus; and this is the spirit of prophecy." (*Teachings of the Prophet Joseph Smith,* p. 160.)

Our eternal salvation will become a reality only as we stay true to our covenants with the Lord. The only way we can stay true and survive the fiery darts of the adversary is to have personal revelation that the path we follow is right and true. Elder Bruce R. McConkie gave this promise: "If we build our house of salvation on the rock of personal revelation, if we build it on the revealed reality that Jesus is the Lord, if we build it on him who is the Eternal Rock—it will stand forever" (*Ensign,* May 1981, p. 77).

Clearly each and every one of us must know for ourselves through personal revelation the reality of our salvation through Jesus Christ. We must work to obtain such if we ever hope to acquire an eternal kingdom with God and his Son, Jesus Christ.

22

True Friendship

What True Friendship Is Not

1. A true friend will not try to persuade us to lower our values. Elder Marvin J. Ashton described true friendship when he said:

> There seems to be a misunderstanding on the part of some men today as to what it means to be a friend. Acts of a friend should result in self-improvement, better attitudes, self-reliance, comfort, consolation, self-respect, and better welfare. Certainly the word friend is misused if it is identified with a person who contributes to our delinquency, misery, and heartaches. (Conference Report, October 1972, pp. 32–33.)

When friends try to get us to lower our standards, they are thinking mostly about themselves. Sometimes young men or young women tell the person they are dating that they love them and ask them to prove their love by violating the moral law. If young men and young women truly cared about their dating companions, they would do everything they could to protect their companion's virtue, not ask them to give it up as a sign of devotion.

This principle applies to all areas of the gospel. Good friends help their friends become better.

2. True friendship is not being loyal in wrongdoing. Elder Richard L. Evans taught that:

> Many have gone the wrong way by following people who were going the wrong way. Sometimes loyalty is given as the reason— but is one really loyal when he is disloyal to his better self, or disloyal to the law? Is one really loyal when he disregards what is good? Following the wrong people to the wrong places may not be an act of loyalty at all. Indeed, we may be much more loyal when we refuse to follow people to the wrong places, because if we don't follow them, they may think more earnestly about their own errors and turn back from what they shouldn't do or where they shouldn't go. (*Improvement Era,* November 1965, p. 1040.)

This counsel was demonstrated by a young woman who became more and more involved with drugs until she suffered an overdose and almost died. She was placed in a rehabilitation clinic, and after many months of pain and struggle she overcame her desire for drugs. Because of her background, many young women would approach her for help with their drug problems.

She realized that these girls would never be able to give up drugs without counseling and help, and she made the decision to be the best friend these girls could have. She would tell them that if they did not tell their parents about their problem, she would contact the parents herself. Many became angry with her and told her they would hate her for the rest of their lives if she told their parents, but she would not back down. She had decided to be a true friend and do what was best for the girls even if they hated her. To this young woman, what her friends thought about her was not as important as doing what was best for them. After receiving the help they needed, many of these girls came back to her and thanked her for her friendship. They had come to realize that she was a true friend after all. Their other friends had done nothing to help them and in many cases even encouraged them to continue their drug use.

What True Friendship Is

1. True friendship can best be taught and practiced in the home. Not only will these friendships bind the family closer together, they will become the foundation for successful relationships outside of the home. One such relationship was described by a young woman in a stake conference in Canada.

> This girl felt homely, but a good friend told her she was beautiful. When there were dances, he would dance with her. "He was handsome and popular, and he lived his religion," she recalls.
> "It was a good thing that he was a strong member of the Church," she said, "because I tailed him everywhere he went. I did what he did. . . . I cannot express the love and respect I have for him. I was not his girlfriend, but I sure loved him. He is on a mission now, and we write regularly. He still loves me and is still my best friend. He is my older brother." (Ron R. Munns, *Ensign*, October 1992, p. 18.)

2. The foundation of true friendship is love and unselfishness. As we become more like the Savior, our capacity to be a good friend increases. The kind of unselfishness that leads to genuine friendship was exhibited by a high school basketball player named Trisha Garn. Her basketball team was playing for the state championship, and she was always the first player off the bench. However, this game was different, and she only played a few seconds of the entire championship game. A sophomore player named Jodi Rees played in her place. The game was a close one, and Jodi played the game of her life while Trisha cheered for her from the bench.

When their team pulled out a win in the last few seconds of play, the crowd erupted. When they cut down the nets, Jodi's dad was asked to cut the last string. A team member explains the great lesson that she learned that day:

> Finally, the net hung by one, lonely string. Hal Rees, Jodi's dad, had the honor of cutting it. He struggled awkwardly up the ladder and, gripping the scissors firmly, managed to snip the last piece.

As the net dropped to the floor tears rolled down the cheeks of our Morgan fans, and when it was placed around Mr. Rees's neck, members of the Rees family held each other tight.

I soon came to understand why Jodi had played more than Trisha. . . . It was because our friend and teammate had done the most unselfish thing possible—she had asked Coach to let Jodi have her playing time. Trisha Garn understood what many in the room didn't. Jodi's 40-year-old dad would not live to see her play again. He was dying of a cancerous brain tumor.

Trisha's selfless act and the sight of Hal hugging Jodi really put our state championship in perspective for me. Sure, it was nice to have the honors of men, but compared to eternal matters of family and Christlike love it didn't seem so significant. . . .

Two-and-a-half weeks after the game, Jodi's dad died. At his funeral the song "Wind beneath My Wings" was sung. Every time I hear the line from that song "Did you ever know that you were my hero?" I think of Trisha. She is my hero. And she'd probably say, "No big deal." But it's a big deal to me. (Liisa London, *New Era,* March 1991, pp. 12–14.)

3. True friendship often leads others into greater church activity. Such was the case with nine young men who all belonged to the same ward. These young men grew up together, but as they started attending high school, four of them became involved with youth who exerted a negative influence on their religious beliefs. They began to miss their church meetings and do other things that were not in accordance with the teachings of the Church. The following story explains what the five active friends did to help their friends through this difficult period of their lives:

They decided to plan some special activity each week to involve their wayward buddies. They also agreed to do all they could to encourage their friends to keep the Word of Wisdom. The friendship that bound these young men together allowed those who were strong in the faith to encourage those who were temporarily weak. Eight of the nine young men later served honorable missions, and all were married in the temple.

The friendship continued through the years. Each summer the nine friends and their families meet to renew their friendship and to recommit themselves to help each other in their quest for eternal life. (Robert B. Arnold, *Church News,* 9 March 1991, p. 7.)

4. True friendship includes being one of our own best friends. Sister Patricia T. Holland taught this important aspect of friendship to the students at Brigham Young University when she said:

My deepest, most earnest wish for you is that you will approach this year with peace and self-assurance—that you will be more caring for yourself and as kind to yourself as you would be to a friend in need. *You* are in need, and you ought to be your own best friend.

When I was your age (and sometimes even now), there was often a struggle over how I saw myself. I was very "skilled" in the art of pummeling myself. . . . So as an old casualty myself, I plead with you to make a distinction between your problems and yourselves—there is a crucial difference. Problems can be painful and dark and disappointing—but *we* are not painful and dark and disappointing. We are children of God and must see ourselves as God sees us, recognizing the positive in ourselves, the part God loves so much. (*BYU 1988–89 Devotional and Fireside Speeches,* p. 23.)

Until we become a good friend to ourselves, we will find being a great friend to others difficult. As we come to accept ourselves as children of God, we feel the confidence to support and help those we associate with. Everyone makes mistakes, and all of us have things to repent of, but dwelling too much on the negative can keep the positive from happening.

5. True friendship is qualifying to be called a friend of the Savior's. Throughout the scriptures he shares his desire to be our friend—to share comfort, strength, guidance, and peace with us. With Jesus as our friend, we can resist any temptation and overcome every problem. Elder Charles Didier invited us to seek the Savior's friendship when he said:

One of the real purposes of life is to become a friend of the Mediator, our Savior and Redeemer, and not only understand his mission but also support it and then qualify to be called his friend, his disciple, and to enter into the presence of his Father. . . .

. . . Are we strong enough to refuse to be a friend of the world and its representatives? Are we strong enough to accept friendship with Christ? Is to be a friend to be complacent and surrender to lower standards, or is it to maintain Christlike standards and defend them? . . . Why not become his disciple by being his witness? . . . Be committed to be his friend! (*Ensign,* November 1983, p. 24.)

23

Prayer

What Prayer Is Not

1. Prayer is not something we should be afraid to do. The story is told of an ancient people who took prisoners sentenced to die into a deep, dark dungeon. In a dark hallway of that dungeon, the prisoners were given two choices. They could either choose to die by hanging or they could choose to open a door at the end of the hallway and meet their unknown fate. Most of the prisoners chose to die by hanging. In the terrors of their imaginations, they conjured up frightening possibilities lying behind the closed door. The sad thing was that the door led to freedom.

The same is true of prayer: it is our door to freedom. Many people, however, are afraid to open the door of prayer. They have many reasons for being hesitant. "He won't listen to me." "I'm not good enough—he knows all the bad things I have done and will be angry." "He couldn't possibly hear all the prayers being offered at once." Sadly, these and many other excuses keep people from praying.

Those who have enough courage to open the door to Heavenly Father through prayer open the door to many good things in life. Prayer can help us to escape from sin and enter a new way of life.

Heavenly Father stands behind the door and welcomes us with open arms.

2. Prayer is not a wish list. Prayer is a time to go to God for comfort, counsel, and direction. Requests are an important part of prayer, but those petitions need to be done the proper way. Elder Neal A. Maxwell described the necessary steps when he wrote:

> Petitioning in prayer has taught me, again and again, that the vault of heaven with all its blessings is to be opened only by a combination lock. One tumbler falls when there is faith, a second when there is personal righteousness; the third and final tumbler falls only when what is sought is, in God's judgment—not ours—right for us. Sometimes we pound on the vault door for something we want very much and wonder why the door does not open. We would be very spoiled children if that vault door opened any more easily than it does. I can tell, looking back, that God truly loves me by inventorying the petitions He has refused to grant me. Our rejected petitions tell us much about ourselves but also much about our flawless Father. (*New Era,* April 1978, p. 6.)

As we pray, it would be well to remember the Lord's attitude of "Not my will, but thine, be done" (Luke 22:42).

3. Prayer is not a waste of time. Many times we think we don't have time to pray. Such was the case one early Sunday morning as Mike and Beth rushed to get themselves and their six-month-old baby ready for stake conference. Mike had been asked to serve as an usher, which required them to be there one half hour before the conference started.

They both got up early and started to get ready. They had planned plenty of time so they wouldn't be late. As the rushing to get ready picked up speed, both Beth and Mike thought about their morning prayers. They concluded that they didn't have time right then and postponed their prayers. They rationalized that perhaps there would be time just before they were to leave.

That plan quickly unraveled as a series of events hacked away at their time. First, an unexpected phone call from Beth's sister who lived out of state tied up her already rushed schedule. But Mike picked up the baby and got him ready—until a power outage sent him scrambling for flashlights. When the time was totally gone, they felt a bit guilty as they rushed out the door without prayer. Two steps away from the front door, the baby spit up all over his Sunday outfit. Beth attempted to wipe it up but could see that he really needed his clothes changed; with a huff, she charged back into the house and made the change.

In tandem, they rushed to the car. Mike quickly backed into the street as he simultaneously checked for cars. His mind saw the unexpected car as his foot hit the brakes, but the slick roads offered little friction as the oncoming car slid into the side of their car. Fortunately, no one was injured, but Mike and Beth's car was damaged so badly that it could not be driven.

Waiting for the police to arrive, both Mike and Beth realized where they had made their mistake. Mike knew that a prayer would have helped him to look sooner and back slower. Beth knew that a prayer would have saved many hassles that morning. They both knew that they may have been a few minutes late getting to stake conference, but as it was they never even got to stake conference. Instead, they spent the rest of the day making arrangements to get their car towed and finding other transportation. They spent many hours over the next month getting the car fixed and working with the insurance company. Mike and Beth learned a valuable lesson that day. They learned that taking time to pray is not a waste of time. In the long run it saves time—and often much more. We must never forget that there is always time to pray.

4. Prayer is not a one-way conversation. It is not a time for us to do all the talking. Genuine prayer is a two-way conversation between Heavenly Father and us. To make it so, we must take time to listen. When we pray we need to pause and listen for what Heavenly Father has to say. President Spencer W. Kimball described it this way:

> Is prayer only one-way communication? No! . . . At the end of our prayers, we need to do some intense listening—even for several minutes. We have prayed for counsel and help. . . .
>
> . . . Sometimes ideas flood our mind as we listen after our prayers. Sometimes feelings press upon us. A spirit of calmness assures us that all will be well. But always, if we have been honest and earnest, we will experience a good feeling—a feeling of warmth for our Father in Heaven and a sense of his love for us. (*Ensign,* October 1981, p. 5.)

What Prayer Is

1. Prayer is a commandment. Elder Marion G. Romney stated: "No divine commandment has been more frequently repeated than the commandment to pray in the name of the Lord Jesus Christ" (*Ensign,* November 1979, p. 16). Prayer is so important that Satan and his followers spend myriad hours encouraging us not to pray. Nephi taught:

> If ye would hearken unto the Spirit which teacheth a man to pray ye would know that ye must pray; for the evil spirit teacheth not a man to pray, but teacheth him that he must not pray.
>
> But behold, I say unto you that ye must pray always, and not faint; that ye must not perform any thing unto the Lord save in the first place ye shall pray unto the Father in the name of Christ, that he will consecrate thy performance unto thee, that thy performance may be for the welfare of thy soul. (2 Nephi 32:8–9.)

2. Prayer involves sincere, continual communication with God. The Lord has counseled us that we should "pray always" (see D&C 10:5). Our hearts should always be in an attitude of prayer. Amulek taught us how and what we should pray for when he stated:

> Cry unto him in your houses, yea, over all your household, both morning, mid-day, and evening.
>
> Yea, cry unto him against the power of your enemies.
>
> Yea, cry unto him against the devil, who is an enemy to all righteousness.
>
> Cry unto him over the crops of your fields, that ye may prosper in them.
>
> Cry over the flocks of your fields, that they may increase.
>
> But this is not all; ye must pour out your souls in your closets, and your secret places, and in your wilderness.
>
> Yea, and when you do not cry unto the Lord, let your hearts be full, drawn out in prayer unto him continually for your welfare, and also for the welfare of those who are around you. (Alma 34:21–27.)

Amulek's repeated use of the word *cry* would indicate more than just a casual attempt at communicating with God. Prayer takes our full attention to return any dividends.

"Prayer is the soul's sincere desire, / Uttered or unexpressed, / The motion of a hidden fire / That trembles in the breast" (*Hymns,* 1985, no. 145).

24

Family Home Evening

What Family Home Evening Is Not

Family home evening is not a way to punish our children for being members of our family. Family home evening should be enjoyable—even *fun!* When we asked teenagers what they felt was the most difficult thing about family home evening, the number one answer given was listening to the lesson. Other responses included "it is sometimes boring," "getting everyone there," and "keeping Dad's comments short."

When we asked teenagers what they liked best about family home evening, the top two answers were refreshments and being together as a family. Other positives mentioned were learning about the gospel and enjoying a game or an activity together.

What Family Home Evening Is

1. Family home evening is a time to enjoy one another. Making home evening enjoyable should be one of our top priorities. In many

families the children ask to have family home evening because they enjoy their time together as a family. This includes both teenagers and younger children. Unless it is enjoyable, home evening will become too much of a hassle or children will be forced to participate and the spirit of home evening will be lost. Here are a few things that successful families do to make home evening more effective and enjoyable.

These families plan lessons for the older children and find ways to include the younger ones. By keeping the lesson short (five to fifteen minutes), the younger children do well. They can be drawing something to do with the lesson or be kept involved in numerous other ways. Many times, because the lesson material is interesting, the children themselves will lengthen the lesson, but that should be a natural outgrowth of the discussion, not part of the lesson plan.

These families plan some kind of game or activity for every home evening, and they don't forget the most important part of home evening—the treats.

Many families take turns preparing and conducting home evening. Even young children can work with an older adult and be involved. (This helps keep Dad from becoming too boring or long-winded.)

Variety adds to the enjoyment of home evenings. This includes such activities as role playing, drawing pictures, watching videos, telling stories, and using object lessons.

2. Family home evening is a vital tool in teaching our children the gospel. Parents have the major responsibility for teaching their children the gospel. The Church auxiliaries play a secondary or backup role to the parents. The importance of parents teaching their children was emphasized by President Spencer W. Kimball when he warned:

Parents should not leave the training of children to others.

There seems to be a growing tendency to shift this responsibility from the home to outside influences such as the school and the church, and of greater concern, to various child-care agencies and institutions. Important as these outward influences may be, they never can adequately take the place of the influence of the mother and the father. Constant training, constant vigilance, companionship, and being watchmen of our own children are necessary in order to keep our homes intact and to bless our children in the Lord's own way. (*Ensign,* May 1979, p. 5.)

Parents teach their children daily through the words they utter, the choices they make, and the examples they set, but home evening gives parents an opportunity to teach in a more formal setting. Prayers, songs, and other preparations help families to discuss things on a deeper spiritual level. The importance of the family in the teaching process was emphasized by Elder James E. Faust when he said, "I am persuaded that family activities can be more effective in fostering the eternal values of love, honesty, chastity, industry, self-worth, and personal integrity than any other institution" (*BYU 1989–90 Devotional and Fireside Speeches,* p. 33).

3. Family home evening is inspired by the Lord. When it is conducted properly, it will bring great blessings to our families. Almost eighty years ago, the First Presidency made a promise that is still in effect today:

> If the Saints obey this counsel [hold weekly family home evening], we promise that great blessings will result. Love at home and obedience to parents will increase. Faith will be developed in the hearts of the youth of Israel, and they will gain power to combat the evil influences and temptations which beset them. (*Improvement Era,* April 1915, pp. 733–34.)

When prophets of God make such promises we can be assured that when we do our part they will come to pass. Some families overlook this great resource because they underestimate the power that home evening can have on their families. This power to change lives was identified by Brother George Durrant. While working on a graduate degree, he conducted a study concerning family home evening and its influence on family members. He chose twenty-five families who had seldom if ever held home evening and asked them to conduct family home evening regularly for three months. The families received many positive blessings, but one family in particular experienced a great change in their lives.

This family consisted of a husband and wife and five young children. During his first visit with the family, Brother Durrant noticed that the father smoked a pipe and had a can of beer close to his chair. He was willing, however, to conduct a weekly family home evening, and his wife and children seemed excited about the prospect. Brother

Durrant returned three months later and asked the family if they had met every week during the last three months. The following conversation then took place.

> The father looked at me intently and said, "I'm not sure. Most weeks we did, but there was one week we aren't sure if what we did was a family home evening or not."
>
> I was pleased at their faithfulness and said, "Well, if you had one every week but one, that's pretty good."
>
> The mother then said, "I think we could even count what we did that week. Anyway, we wanted to ask you if what we did would count."
>
> I said, "Tell me what you did and we'll see."
>
> The father replied, "That's the week we went to the temple to be sealed together forever as a family." His eyes were moist with tears as he asked, "Can we count that?"
>
> I was caught off-guard by this unexpected response and I could hardly speak because of emotion. I softly replied, "Yes, I believe we could count that."
>
> The mother's eyes and face shone as she said, "We went to the temple on my birthday."
>
> He quickly added, "I couldn't even get her much of a present. Since we started paying tithing, there's not much money left over for presents."
>
> Tears fell freely from his wife's face as she looked into his eyes and said, "When you took me to the temple, that was the best present that I've ever received because that's what I wanted more than anything else in the world."
>
> By now the children all wanted to tell me about the temple and what going there meant to them. After listening to their happy reports, I asked the father, "What happened to cause this mighty change?"
>
> His simple reply was, "Well, I did what you said. Each week I'd call my family together and we'd have family home evening. After a few weeks, I saw the children sitting there real close to me and their mother. We all felt so good and so happy. I just decided it was time we started changing things. We talked about going to the

temple so that we could be together forever. We talked to our home teachers and then to the bishop. And in a few weeks we felt we were worthy to go to the temple." (*Love at Home—Starring Father,* pp. 11–13.)

When we do those things that God wants us to do, great power is unleashed in our behalf. The power of the gospel can transform our thoughts and actions—our very lives. It should not be surprising to us that Elder Dallin H. Oaks said that "family home evening is the ideal time to accomplish almost every type of family togetherness. It is the ideal place for the family to pray together, learn together, counsel together, play together, and even work together. Most of us recognize this, but I wonder how many of us are really using the family home evening to its full potential." (*Ensign,* June 1985, pp. 10–11.)

4. Home evening helps our families live the gospel better. Some families don't hold family home evening, because they feel their children are being taught the gospel at Church. Other families zero in on the doctrine in home evening but spend little time discussing or promoting its application. Home evening is a place where family members can learn to apply the gospel.

Let's discuss the law of love, for example. Most of us know that Jesus said that to love God and our fellowmen is the most important thing we can do, yet many of our homes suffer from a lack of this love. In these situations, a lesson about love is not as important as focusing on how to better apply love in the family. One family taught such a lesson by having each family member "recall a time when his or her behavior showed a lack of love. Then each role-played how he would have acted had he been showing love. They concluded that each of them could live Christ's law of love more perfectly, and each worked out some specific changes he or she was going to make." (*Ensign,* February 1987, p. 19.)

Since that time, each family member has been trying harder to live the law of love, and the results have been rewarding. As children and parents learn to better live the gospel principles at home, they find themselves also applying them in public. Through careful discussion, study, and prayer, families can choose and teach home evening lessons that will increase the spirituality and happiness of our homes.

25

Humility

What Humility Is Not

1. Humility is not found in Satan or his followers. A possible definition for humility might be: To know that there is a God and that you are not him.

Before the War in Heaven, Satan stepped forward with his plan. It would force all into submission, which was contrary to the teachings of our Heavenly Father. Backed by a third part of the hosts of heaven, he became a god unto himself. By thinking he knew more than God, he confined himself and his followers to everlasting misery.

Today, he and his followers spend their energies bringing others down to their state of unhappiness. All that he promotes is centered in the opposite of humility—pride. He whispers to us such statements as: "No one has the right to tell you what to do"; "What you do with your life is your business"; and "Your education makes you smarter than the prophets." This self-serving, pride-filled attitude can lead only to unhappiness. Unhappiness is always the result of becoming our own god or making Satan our god.

The first step in gaining humility is to recognize that God and his prophets and servants are wiser than we are and then to follow them.

As we follow their counsel, we set ourselves up to enjoy the rich blessings of joy and happiness that Heavenly Father has to give.

2. Humility is not easy to develop. King Benjamin taught:

> The natural man is an enemy to God, and has been from the fall of Adam, and will be, forever and ever, unless he yields to the enticings of the Holy Spirit, and putteth off the natural man and becometh a saint through the atonement of Christ the Lord, and becometh as a child, submissive, meek, humble, patient, full of love, willing to submit to all things which the Lord seeth fit to inflict upon him, even as a child doth submit to his father (Mosiah 3:19).

Our natural desire is to be proud and self-centered. It takes work to humble ourselves and admit that we are not the source of all knowledge and understanding. At times divine intervention must help us overcome the pride of our heart. One of the great messages of the Book of Mormon is that man's natural tendency is to forget who is the source of all good things. We read of great societies that prospered, only to fall because of pride. They failed to recognize God as the giver of all the good in their lives.

An example of man's natural tendency to forget God was demonstrated during a recent Academy Awards ceremony. An individual kept track of the "thanks" given by those receiving an Oscar. There were fifty-nine expressions of gratitude given to people such as producers, co-workers, and friends, six to family, and only one to God.

Elder Marvin J. Ashton taught:

> How easy it is for man to believe that temporal success has been achieved by his own skills and labor. Everything good comes from the Lord. . . .
>
> It pleases God to have us humbly recognize his powers and his influence in our accomplishments rather than to indicate by words or innuendo that we have been responsible for remarkable achievements. . . .
>
> . . . Humility must be our foundation if the goodness of the Lord is to continue to come to and from us. (*Ensign,* May 1990, pp. 66–67.)

It was interesting to watch on television a few years ago as one of the really successful United States space shuttle flights landed. As the spacecraft touched down, the announcer in his excitement exclaimed, "There is nothing we can't do!" How sad it was a few months later when the space shuttle exploded, killing the astronauts aboard. The words "There is nothing we can't do" rang sickeningly to the ear.

We read in the Doctrine and Covenants: "And in nothing doth man offend God, or against none is his wrath kindled, save those who confess not his hand in all things, and obey not his commandments" (D&C 59:21).

What Humility Is

1. Humility is found in Jesus Christ.

> Humility is royalty without a crown,
> Greatness in plain clothes,
> Erudition without decoration,
> Wealth without display,
> Power without scepter or force,
> Position demanding no preferential rights,
> Greatness sitting in the congregation,
> Prayer in closets and not in corners of the street,
> Fasting in secret without publication,
> Stalwartness without a label,
> Supplication upon its knees.
> Divinity riding an ass.
>
> (Spencer W. Kimball, *Improvement Era,* August 1963, p. 704.)

The Savior is our exemplar of true humility. He was the greatest individual to ever walk the earth, yet he took no honor to himself but gave all the glory to the Father. He sought and willingly followed all the Father commanded. We should take the Savior as our guide and emulate his humility.

2. Humility is knowing we are nothing without God and others. Joseph Smith understood and taught this when he stated: "The greatest temporal and spiritual blessings which always come from faithfulness and concerted effort, never attended individual exertion or enterprise" (*Teachings of the Prophet Joseph Smith,* p. 183).

The sum of who we are and what we have become is not a result of our individual effort alone but rather must include the countless efforts given by God and others in our behalf.

We might not even recognize countless acts of service. The Lord taught us to serve anonymously (see Matthew 6:1–4). It would stand to reason then that he serves us anonymously. We need to develop a habit of thanking him regularly for those countless acts of silent service.

A story is told of a young man from Utah who served during World War II. He was called to serve in an area several time zones away from his home.

He wore on his wrist a watch to tell him the time in the area he was living. But he carried in his pocket an old timepiece that gave another time of day. His buddies noted that frequently he would look at his wristwatch and then at the pocket watch. This strange behavior led them to ask why he had the additional watch. Unembarrassed, he promptly said:

> "The wristwatch tells me the time here where we are, but the big watch which Pa gave me tells me what time it is in UTAH. You see," he continued, "mine is a large family—a very close family. When the big watch says 5 A.M. I know Dad is rolling out to milk the cows. And any night when it says 7:30, I know the whole family is around a well-spread table on their knees thanking the Lord for what's on the table and asking Him to watch over me and keep me clean and honorable. It's those things that make me want to fight when the goin' gets tough. . . . I can find out what time it is here easy enough. What I want to know is what time it is in UTAH." (See Spencer W. Kimball, *Ensign,* July 1973, p. 17; adapted from Vaughn R. Kimball, "The Right Time at Home," *Reader's Digest,* May 1944, p. 43.)

This young soldier humbly recognized and understood the great role his family played in his success. None of us stands alone; all are interdependent on each other for strength and peace. Understanding this fact leaves very little room for pride in our lives.

3. Humility is accepting the fact that we are dependent on grace for our eternal progression. Grace is when someone willingly and without reward does something for us that we cannot do for ourselves. In the gospel there are two kinds of grace. The first and most important type of grace is the divine grace given us through the love of Jesus Christ.

> It is through the grace of the Lord Jesus, made possible by his atoning sacrifice, that mankind will be raised in immortality, every person receiving his body from the grave in a condition of everlasting life. It is likewise through the grace of the Lord that individuals, through faith in the atonement of Jesus Christ and repentance of their sins, receive strength and assistance to do good works that they otherwise would not be able to maintain if left to their own means. This grace is an enabling power that allows men and women to lay hold on eternal life and exaltation after they have expended their own best efforts. (LDS edition of the Bible, Bible Dictionary, p. 697.)

God's grace goes beyond the effects of the Atonement. We recognize that his hand moves in our behalf on many occasions, helping us accomplish many things we would not be able to do on our own. We should thank him daily for his abundant grace.

The second type of grace in the gospel is what might be called human grace. There are times in our lives when the charity and good will of others enables us to do something that we could not do on our own. For instance, a man with heart disease became so debilitated that he lost his job and, with it, his medical benefits. When his disease progressed to the point that he needed a heart transplant, he was overcome with the impossibility of the situation. The cost of the transplant was one hundred and fifty thousand dollars. There was no possible way he could get a heart transplant on his own.

Several family members, friends, and even people he didn't know raised the money needed for the transplant. Several weeks later, a family stepped back from their own grief long enough to think of someone else and donated their deceased loved one's heart for the transplant. This man's life was saved because of the grace of others.

As we recognize the abundance of divine and human grace in our lives, we can only marvel at our blessings. In gratitude and humility we realize that our earthly happiness and our eternal progression would be blocked without having our Savior, our Father, and others by our side.

26

Forgiving Others

What Forgiving Others Is Not

Forgiving others is not allowing feelings of animosity or resentment to fester in our hearts. We are counseled to "rejoice not when thine enemy falleth, and let not thine heart be glad when he stumbleth" (Proverbs 24:17).

The Lord gave the pattern for true forgiveness when he said, "He who has repented of his sins, the same is forgiven, and I, the Lord, remember them no more" (D&C 58:42). The Lord has not actually forgotten what we have done as much as he no longer holds our offensive actions against us. Forgiveness is closely linked to charity, the pure love of Christ. We forgive because we love everyone as a son or daughter of God. When we have truly forgiven a person, we feel good about their successes and desire to help them be happy.

What Forgiving Others Is

1. Forgiveness is necessary to be forgiven. When we are willing to forgive others, we appreciate the great gift of forgiveness that the

Savior offers us. He was abused, spit upon, beaten, mocked, and nailed to the cross in our behalf. His love for us was such that he bled from every pore so that we could be forgiven of our sins. No one has offended us or ever will offend us to the degree that Jesus was offended for us.

As part of our effort to be forgiven, Jesus has required that we forgive all those who offend us. Jesus taught us that we should ask God to "forgive us of our debts, *as* we forgive our debtors" (Matthew 6:12; italics added). He also warned us that "if ye forgive not men their trespasses, neither will your Father forgive your trespasses" (Matthew 6:15).

It would be hypocritical to expect God to forgive us if we were not willing to forgive others. Jesus identified this problem in the parable of the servant who was forgiven of a huge debt by the king and then refused to forgive a man who owed him a paltry one hundred pence (see Matthew 18:23–35). The offenses we have committed against God are enormous compared to the offenses that have been committed against us. To not forgive others reveals a stingy and ungrateful heart.

2. Forgiveness demonstrates humility and true brotherly love. Jesus taught this aspect of forgiveness in the famous parable of the prodigal son. When the son finally came to his senses and returned to his father, instead of being happy for him his brother resented the attention that the prodigal received. When the father saw his older son's refusal to forgive, he explained to him, "It was meet that we should make merry, and be glad: for this thy brother was dead, and is alive again; and was lost, and is found" (Luke 15:32).

We never find out if the brother's heart is softened by these words, but the message is clear. Every person that ever offends us is literally a brother or a sister, and we should feel jubilation and joy when they respond to our Father's message. In the meantime we should feel a desire to help them return rather than a hope that "they get theirs."

3. Forgiveness brings spiritual growth and helps us become more like God. An unforgiving attitude releases into our souls the poisons of bitterness, hate, envy, and malice, which drive the Spirit of the Lord out of our lives. Referring to this spiritual canker, Bishop H. Burke Peterson said: "The longer the poison of resentment and unforgiveness stays in a body, the greater and longer lasting is its destructive force. . . . The poison of revenge, or of unforgiving thoughts or attitudes,

unless removed, will destroy the soul in which it is harbored."
(*Ensign,* November 1983, p. 59.)

The growth that comes when we purge our souls through forgiveness was experienced by a man who had been called to be a mission president. Years before, his father and his father's cousin had become business competitors in the same community. They had become bitter toward one another and passed on these feelings to their sons. This same bitterness still existed between him and his cousin even though they both served as bishops of their respective wards.

The call to be a mission president brought with it uneasy feelings concerning his relationship with his cousin. He finally responded to the Spirit and went to his cousin's home. This man tells what happened next:

When I rang the doorbell he invited me into the living room and congratulated me on my mission call. We talked a few minutes about things in general, and then it happened. I looked at him with a feeling of love which replaced all the old bitterness, and said: "I have come to ask forgiveness for anything I have ever said or done that has tended to divide us and our families."

At this point tears came into our eyes, and for a few minutes neither of us could say a word. This was one time when silence was more powerful than words. In a few minutes he said: "I wish I had come to you first." I replied, "The important thing is that it is done, not who initiated it."

At this moment we had a rich spiritual experience which caused us to purge our lives and our souls of those things which had separated us. That experience has resulted in our having proper family relationships. Now I could go on my mission and teach the true meaning of love because for the first time in my life I had experienced its deepest dimension. Now I could honestly say that there wasn't a person in the world that I didn't love and appreciate. Since that day my life has never been the same, for it was then that I learned in a most positive way, as I had never understood before, this injunction of the Master to his disciples: "A new commandment I give unto you, That ye love one another" (John 13:34). (*Ensign,* July 1980, p. 4.)

God wants us to forgive—for our sakes—even if the offender doesn't seem to deserve it. Because of his great love for us, he asks us to forgive everyone so that our souls will be poison free and remain accessible to the promptings and guidance of the Spirit. We bless ourselves more than anyone else when we forgive.

4. Forgiving others allows us to help those who have offended us. Those who injure and insult others are wrestling with spiritual and emotional problems that are keeping them from being happy. As we learn to love others and overlook their inappropriate words and actions, many times the Spirit will prompt us into action on their behalf. We will receive guidance concerning what we can say or do that will not only heal the division among us but will also help heal their grieving soul. When someone offends another, both of the people involved have a problem. An experience from the life of President George Albert Smith illustrates this point.

When he was a young man, George Albert ran for an office in the Utah National Guard. His opponent was a man whom he considered his friend, but this man spread lies about George Albert in order to win. Because of the lies, George Albert lost the election and the promotion that accompanied it.

George Albert went to church and tried to forget about what had happened, but his heart was filled with hate and bitterness, and he found that he did not feel right about taking the sacrament. Through meditation and prayer, he came to realize that he was in the wrong for feeling the way he did. Here is an account of what happened next.

He decided to relieve himself of the burden of hate that seemed to be doing him more harm than it was doing his enemy. He crossed the street and walked directly into the office of the man who had spread the rumors. As he entered the door, the man put up his arm as if in self-defense. No doubt he expected a fight. He knew in his heart that he had gravely wronged a friend. But George Albert Smith had not come to fight. On the contrary, his voice was soft and forgiving.

"My brother," he said, "I want you to forgive me for hating you the way I have for the last few weeks."

The man of rumors was immediately melted into contrition. "Brother Smith," he said, "you have no need for forgiveness. It is

I who need forgiveness from you." Because of George Albert Smith's courage and spiritual strength, the man who had made himself an enemy was completely subdued. He repented of his evil conduct and thereafter he and Brother Smith were once more good friends. (*Instructor,* June 1965, p. 232.)

More important than these two men becoming friends again was the spiritual help this man received through George Albert Smith's efforts. His actions had driven the Spirit from his life, and no man is happy in this condition. Because of George Albert's willingness to forgive and reach out to him, this man repented of his sins and made himself right with God again.

Even though some offenders may not respond as willingly to our attempts to make things right, we still have an obligation to reach out to them. As we purge negative feelings from our own hearts, we position ourselves to help others overcome their problems.

5. God will give us the power to forgive others. He will help us completely purge negative feelings, such as malice and hatred, from our hearts. For many of us, God's command to forgive *all* offenses is one of the most difficult things we have been asked to do. It is helpful, and even vital, to remember that we are not alone. God has promised us that when we do our best he will intercede and give us the power to overcome any problem and obey any commandment (see 1 Nephi 3:7). Paul said it another way when he promised, "God is faithful, who will not suffer you to be tempted above that ye are able; but will with the temptation also make a way to escape, that ye may be able to bear it" (1 Corinthians 10:13).

Christl Fechter, a Czechoslovakian refugee, discovered the truth of this promise when she faced a situation that she could not overcome alone. She was forced to leave her homeland for Germany, where she was taught the gospel and joined the Church. A year later she moved to Bountiful, Utah. Here she was terribly hurt emotionally and for the first time in her life felt hatred. The following story explains how, with the help of the Lord, she was able to overcome her hate and bitterness:

"I had been through all the terrors of the invasion of my country, but I had never before experienced the feeling of hate," she says. "It changed my personality. Even my nonmember friends realized that I was not the same person any more. I knew this feeling was wrong, but I did not know how to change it."

One day Christl read in Matthew 5:43–45 of Jesus' command to love our enemies and even pray for them. She felt that this passage had been written just for her.

"I could not imagine myself praying for this person, but I wanted to do what the Lord said, and I knew I had to get rid of the hatred," she says. So she knelt that night and prayed, with reservations, that the Lord would bless the person who had hurt her.

She felt a little better. The next night she prayed again, this time wholeheartedly, and she immediately felt the hatred lift from her, never to return. She discovered that the Lord could pour out his Spirit upon her and teach her to love as he does. (*Ensign,* June 1988, p. 53.)

God is no respecter of persons. He will not refuse to help us in our efforts to forgive and love others. As we turn to him wholeheartedly, as Christl did, he will bless us also and we will be able to feel this love. There may be nothing we do here upon this earth that makes us more like God than loving our enemies and forgiving those who offend us.

27

Honesty

What Honesty Is Not

1. $\mathbf{H}$onesty is not something that changes with circumstances. As Joseph Smith worked on the translation of the Book of Mormon, Martin Harris served as his scribe. After Joseph translated 116 pages of written manuscript, Martin wanted to take the manuscript and show it to others as proof of what he and Joseph were doing. After counseling with the Lord, Joseph reluctantly allowed Martin to take the manuscript. The pages were lost and never returned to the Prophet. The Lord knew what had happened to the manuscript and revealed it to Joseph. In section 10 of the Doctrine and Covenants, the Lord instructed Joseph not to retranslate that portion of the plates from which the 116 pages of manuscript originated because the manuscript had fallen into the hands of evil men whom Satan inspired to alter the words. Their plan was to wait for Joseph to retranslate the information and then to bring forth their altered manuscript and say that Joseph was a fraud. The Lord then made a very important statement about honesty:

> And thus he [Satan] has laid a cunning plan, thinking to destroy the work of God; but I will require this at their hands, and it

shall turn to their shame and condemnation in the day of judgment.

Yea, he stirreth up their hearts to anger against this work.

Yea, he saith unto them: Deceive and lie in wait to catch, that ye may destroy; behold, this is no harm. And thus he flattereth them, and telleth them that it is no sin to lie that they may catch a man in a lie, that they may destroy him. (D&C 10:23–25.)

The Lord made it clear that lying is always dishonest. Satan would want us to believe that we are still being honest if there is a good reason for lying. However, that kind of reasoning cannot be further from truth. The Lord desires us to be honest under all circumstances.

If we ever hope to become like God, we must be totally honest. If God lied, he would cease to be God. The brother of Jared understood this when he said, "Yea, Lord, I know that thou speakest the truth, for thou art a God of truth, and canst not lie" (Ether 3:12). Enos also stated, "And I, Enos, knew that God could not lie; wherefore, my guilt was swept away" (Enos 1:6).

Elder Marvin J. Ashton has never forgotten the definition of honesty that a special teacher gave him while he was a young boy: "A lie is any communication given to another with the intent to deceive." He explained that this teacher also repeated often the words: "Don't tell lies. Don't share lies. Don't participate in lies." (See *Ensign,* May 1982, p. 9.)

2. Honesty is not easy. Another lie that Satan, the father of all lies, would have us believe is that honesty is too hard. He would have us accept the fantasy that it is all right to lie a little and that nothing serious will result. Nephi foresaw this malady that would abide with us in the last days:

And there shall also be many which shall say: Eat, drink, and be merry; nevertheless, fear God—he will justify in committing a little sin; yea, lie a little, take the advantage of one because of his words, dig a pit for thy neighbor; there is no harm in this; and do all these things, for tomorrow we die; and if it so be that we are guilty, God will beat us with a few stripes, and at last we shall be saved in the kingdom of God (2 Nephi 28:8).

Real honesty takes hard work and courage. The opposite is true for lying. "Lies are often excuses for lack of courage. Sometimes lies are nothing more than excuses for poor performance." (Marvin J. Ashton, *Ensign,* May 1982, p. 10.)

Elder Hartman Rector, Jr., tells of a young friend who went to take a test in school. He was totally unprepared for the test but still prayed mightily for the Lord to help him. As this friend sat in his classroom seat, who should sit down beside him but the smartest girl in the class. He said to himself, "Well, this must be the answer to my prayer. Here she is. The Lord provided her, right here."

This young returned missionary had been preaching honesty for two years. No sooner had this thought come into his mind than he began to argue with himself. He found it very difficult to go against that which he had been preaching. Between the chaos in his mind and his total lack of preparation, he flunked the test.

Elder Rector then explained:

But as a matter of fact he really passed the test.

You see, he had passed the Lord's test, and that is the test that we have to pass here upon this earth. Tests are all around us. Fifty years from the day that he took the test he would not remember what his grade was on it, and it really would not make any difference so long as it was honest. But if he cheated on the test, he would remember that, for it makes an indelible imprint on the spirit. It also makes it easier the next time you are faced with a temptation where your honesty is in question to go down that broad road. (See *Get Up and Glow,* p. 7.)

Satan's definition of honesty is full of rationalizations and excuses. He promotes the easy way out and would have us take no responsibility for our actions. He wears a mask called honesty, but behind the mask is the real face of deceit—self-serving and devious. One of the famous excuses people use is "the devil made me do it." The devil cannot make us do anything. We have the choice; the problem is that it takes courage and hard work to follow the truth.

When we think of honesty, we should remember the words of the Savior: "Enter ye in at the strait gate: for wide is the gate, and broad is the way, that leadeth to destruction, and many there be which go in threat: because strait is the gate and narrow is the way, which leadeth unto life, and few there be that find it" (Matthew 7:13–14).

What Honesty Is

Honesty is a key to freedom and happiness. The story is told of a man who went one evening to steal corn from a neighbor's field, and he took his son along to sit on the fence as a lookout. The man jumped over the fence with a large bag in his arms. Before taking any corn he looked all around, first one way and then the other. Satisfied that no one was looking, he was just ready to fill his bag when his son yelled, "Dad, there is one way you haven't looked yet." Startled, the man turned around and saw his son pointing up. The man was pricked to his soul, dropped the bag, and humbly went home with his son.

We can hide nothing from God. He sees and knows all that we do. In the Doctrine and Covenants we read: "Hearken, O ye people of my church, saith the voice of him who dwells on high, and whose eyes are upon all men" (D&C 1:1). We only deceive ourselves if we think we are hiding anything from him. Likewise we lie to ourselves if we do not face up to our dishonest acts. We know when we are being honest and what the intent of our heart is. Elder Marvin J. Ashton gave an appropriate question we could ask ourselves: "In all our words and deeds we should ask ourselves, 'Is it right? Is it true?' Not 'Is it expedient, satisfactory, convenient, or profitable?' " (*Ensign,* May 1982, p. 11.)

Real happiness can only come as we gain peace with ourselves and God. That peace is only found by being totally honest with self and God. When a person understands and practices total honesty, he has set himself on the path to real happiness and perfect freedom: "And ye shall know the truth, and the truth shall make you free" (John 8:32).

A good example of the peace and freedom that comes from being honest was related by Jeffrey R. Holland. He described an experience that happened one night when he came home quite late from work. His nine-year-old daughter, Mary, seemed visibly distressed. He asked her if she felt all right; she nodded that she did, but he guessed otherwise. He waited as she got ready for bed. She then walked into the living room and said, "Daddy, I have to talk to you." He held her hand, and as they walked into her bedroom, she started to cry.

She then said, "I was at [the store] this morning and saw a ladies' compact I knew Mother would love. I was sure it was quite expensive, but I picked it up just to admire it. It fell out of my hands onto the floor. I quickly picked it up, but Daddy, the mirror was cracked. I didn't know what to do! I didn't have enough money to pay for it, and I was all alone. . . . I put the compact back on the shelf and left the store. Oh, Daddy, I think I've been dishonest."

Brother Holland held her in his arms, and the little nine-year-old shook with pain as she said, "I can't sleep and I can't eat and I can't say my prayers. What will I do? I won't ever get it out of my mind."

Sister Holland joined her husband, and the two of them talked with their daughter about the compact. They told her that they were very, very proud of her honesty, and they would have been disappointed if she had been able to eat or sleep very well. Brother Holland told her the compact probably wouldn't cost too much and that they would go back to the store manager and tell him of the problem, and between the two of them they could cover the cost. If the compact was still there, perhaps they could buy it for her mother. The cracked mirror could be a reminder for as long as she owned it that her little girl was unfailingly honest and spiritually sensitive.

As they finished the talk, little Mary's tears stopped and she said, "I think now I can say my prayers." (See J. Richard Clarke, *Ensign,* May 1984, pp. 63–64.)

28

The Law of the Fast

Mark and Brenda tried to teach the importance of fasting to their children from the time they were young. When their children were baptized, they suggested to them that they should begin living the law of the fast. To one of their sons, fasting seemed the most difficult thing the Lord had ever asked anyone to do from the time of Adam. Every fast Sunday he would complain about his terrible stomach pain and his horrible headaches. This was not toward the end of the day but within an hour or two of getting out of bed. After three or four hours of acting like a martyr, he would eat a bowl of cereal, and his cries of pain and despair would cease until the next fast Sunday.

When his parents suggested that fasting could bring him closer to God, he replied that he only felt hunger. When they pointed out to him that the money from the missed meals was given to the poor, he suggested that the family was rich enough to eat the two meals and still donate to the poor. Once this young man prayed, studied, and put forth the effort to gain a testimony, he began to fast the right way with the right attitudes, and his fasting became much more beneficial.

Many people suffer through fast day because they do not understand the purpose of fasting and how to make it meaningful in their lives. These people fail to receive many blessings that could be theirs. Before we discuss what fasting can be, here are a few things that fasting is not—or at least shouldn't be.

What Fasting Is Not

1. Fasting cannot be accomplished by force. When not accompanied by prayer, fasting is hardly more than an interval of forced hunger. We can make children go hungry, but we cannot make them fast. This principle was clarified by President Joseph F. Smith when he said:

> I have known children to cry for something to eat on fast day. In such cases, going without food will do them no good. Instead, they dread the day to come, and in place of hailing it, dislike it; while the compulsion engenders a spirit of rebellion in them, rather than a love for the Lord and their fellows. Better teach them the principle, and let them observe it when they are old enough to choose intelligently, than to so compel them. (*Gospel Doctrine,* p. 244.)

2. Fasting is not required of everyone. Some people feel that the Lord requires them to fast even when health reasons indicate this is not a good idea. President Joseph F. Smith said that "many are subject to weakness, others are delicate in health, and others have nursing babies; of such it should not be required to fast" (*Gospel Doctrine,* p. 244).

3. Fasting is not just going without food. You have probably noticed that the drinking fountain in your meetinghouse is kept fairly busy on fast day. This is because some don't realize that fasting is not just going without food for a period of time. Neither food nor drink are supposed to be taken during a normal fast. Some Church leaders have suggested abstinence from physical pleasures in addition to food and drink in order to better focus on the purposes of our fast.

4. Fasting is not walking around with a grouchy face or a tired, run-down look. Jesus taught us that we should fast in such a way that our fasting would not be apparent to others. In the Doctrine and Covenants the Savior used the words *fasting* and *rejoicing* interchangeably (see D&C 59:14). Fast days should be pleasant and enjoyable.

5. Fasting is not interrupted by necessary medicines or the sacrament. Some feel that once they have consumed any liquid or food, they have broken their fast. Since they feel the sacrament ends their fast, they return home to a family meal immediately after fast meeting, even though they might not have fasted the normal amount of time yet. The Church has counseled us that we should fast at least two meals as part of our fast-day worship.

What Fasting Is

Fasting is a form of worship. Through fasting we can seek help from our Heavenly Father or thank him for his generous blessings. Fasting becomes meaningful when we fast for a specific purpose and dedicate the time involved to the Lord. When we are truly fasting, physical needs become unimportant. Instead we meditate and contemplate spiritual things; indeed, pondering and prayer are vital components of fasting.

Many specific reasons for fasting are found in the scriptures. It is appropriate to fast for the sick (see 2 Samuel 12:16), to know the truth (see Acts 10:30–33), to gain a testimony (see Alma 5:46), for direction and guidance (see Omni 1:26), and for comfort (see Alma 28:2–6). Almost anything we might discuss in our prayers could become an object of a fast. The following story illustrates the uncommon and sometimes miraculous results that can come from fasting and prayer.

On Sunday, Oct. 17, the two Church officials met with 698 members of the Tutuila District of the Samoan Mission. As part of the session President Brown dedicated recently completed classrooms and faculty houses.

For many days prior to the visit, members of the school faculty and students at the Church school in American Samoa had been fasting and praying for moisture. Since water supply is totally dependent upon rainfall and the accumulated storage of water, a severe drought had caused the school's reservoir to be drained to the point where emergency measures were being taken.

During the early morning conference session, the heavens opened and literally produced a deluge of rain, fully replenishing the water supply. An airline pilot later commented, "I have scarcely seen such an unusual rainfall. The only place where rainclouds hovered was over this particular segment of American Samoa." Surely those who had been fasting and praying could explain the significance of the unusual storm. (Henry A. Smith, *Church News,* 11 December 1965, p. 6.)

Sometimes we tend to fast for physical needs—such as restoration of health, moisture, and protection—and overlook spiritual needs that may be of even more importance. Isaiah suggested both physical and spiritual purposes for fasting: "Is not this the fast that I have chosen? to loose the bands of wickedness, to undo the heavy burdens, and to let the oppressed go free, and that ye break every yoke? Is it not to deal thy bread to the hungry, and that thou bring the poor that are cast out to thy house?" (Isaiah 58:6–7.)

The Lord has promised great blessings to those who sincerely fast and strive to communicate with him. Fasting is one of the basic ingredients of gaining spiritual power and increasing our self-mastery. Notice the blessings that Isaiah promised those who fast for the right reasons and with the right attitudes:

Then shall thy light break forth as the morning, and thine health shall spring forth speedily: and thy righteousness shall go before thee; the glory of the Lord shall be thy rereward.

Then shalt thou call, and the Lord shall answer; thou shalt cry, and he shall say, Here I am. . . .

And the Lord shall guide thee continually, and satisfy thy soul in drought, and make fat thy bones: and thou shalt be like a watered garden, and like a spring of water, whose waters fail not. (Isaiah 58:8–9, 11.)

Like most gospel principles, the blessings of the fast come in direct relationship to our attitude, effort, and commitment. As we improve in these areas, we receive increasing benefits from our fasting. Fasting truly becomes rejoicing, for we feel God's power and love at work in our lives.

29

Death

One of the saddest and gladdest days in a parent's life is when a child graduates from high school. It is sad because parents know that their son or daughter will be leaving home soon to begin life on his or her own. These parents realize that their home will never be the same without the excitement and energy of their teenager. However, it is a glad day because they are proud of their child's accomplishment. As parents they are full of excitement for the growth and adventure they know lies ahead for their graduate. If asked, most parents would tell you this is a day of great happiness, even though there is some sadness associated with it.

Death has been called a graduation day. In many ways, death is like the earthly graduations we all know so well. Using that comparison, let us consider some things that death is not.

What Death Is Not

1. Death is not final. Elder Wright and Elder Morgan were called by the director of a funeral home and asked if they would conduct a

funeral service at the mortuary for a seventeen-year-old young man. The teenager had been killed in a car accident the day before. He had been baptized a member of the Church when he was fifteen and was the only member of the Church in a family that had no other religious affiliation. As the two elders conducted the funeral services, they taught the principles of the gospel. At the conclusion of the service, the casket was carried to the waiting hearse. Those family members present who had no religious training or belief wailed uncontrollably. The young man's mother fainted and had to be carried to her car. It was indeed a very sad scene. They carried no hope of ever seeing their loved one again. To them, death was final. They knew not the Savior.

Those who know and understand the mission of Jesus Christ know that death is not the end. Christ illuminates the darkness brought by death. Abinadi taught: "There is a resurrection, therefore the grave hath no victory, and the sting of death is swallowed up in Christ. He is the light and the life of the world; yea, a light that is endless, that can never be darkened; yea, and also a life which is endless, that there can be no more death." (Mosiah 16:8–9.)

In the dark hours following the death of a loved one, we should keep foremost in our mind the eternal perspective of death. Elder Neal A. Maxwell put death in its proper place when he stated: "Death is a mere comma, not an exclamation point!" (Conference Report, April 1983, p. 13.)

2. Death is sad, but it is not bad. President Gordon B. Hinckley described it this way: "Death, though bitter to observe, is not the end, but is rather, only another graduation from which we go on to a better life" (*Ensign,* May 1988, p. 65). Death is simply one of the steps in moving us toward exaltation—hardly something bad! President Brigham Young taught:

> We shall turn round and look upon it [the valley of death] and think, when we have crossed it, why this is the greatest advantage of my whole existence, for I have passed from a state of sorrow, grief, mourning, woe, misery, pain, anguish and disappointment into a state of existence where I can enjoy life to the fullest extent as far as that can be done without a body. My spirit is set free, I thirst no more, I want to sleep no more, I hunger no more, I tire no more, I run, I walk, I labor, I go, I come, I do this, I do that, what-

ever is required of me, nothing like pain or weariness, I am full of life, full of vigor, and I enjoy the presence of my Heavenly Father. (*Journal of Discourses,* 17:142.)

A faithful young Latter-day Saint died of a disease that had ravished his body and had taken an emotional toll on family members and friends. At this young man's funeral, one of the speakers issued a challenge to those present. He asked them to make a list of all the reasons we have to die. Such a list is very helpful in understanding what death means to us. A few of those reasons follow.

What Death Is

1. Death is a necessary step in God's plan. Without death there could be no resurrection. Death releases our spirit from our mortal body so that one day we can receive an immortal, glorified body. Many suffer great physical pain before they depart this life. What a blessing to know that they will no longer feel pain and will have the privilege of one day having a perfect body! The Lord described the great benefit of death and the resurrection when he stated: "For man is spirit. The elements are eternal, and spirit and element, inseparably connected, receive a fulness of joy; and when separated, man cannot receive a fulness of joy." (D&C 93:33–34.)

Only through the Resurrection and the Atonement can we have the fulness of joy that Heavenly Father desires for us.

2. Death can increase our love. There is an old saying, "Absence makes the heart grow fonder." The passing of a loved one often increases our appreciation and love for that person. Our temporary separation helps us gain a new perspective of how much we truly love them. When we are reunited, our bond of love can be stronger than ever before.

3. Death reunites us with those whom we know and love. Brigham Young taught that our departure from this life will involve a great reunion with many whom we love: "We have more friends behind the

veil than on this side, and they will hail us more joyfully than you were ever welcomed by your parents and friends in this world; and you will rejoice more when you meet them than you ever rejoiced to see a friend in this life" (*Discourses of Brigham Young,* pp. 379–80).

We read in the Doctrine and Covenants that our association with friends and loved ones will be greatly enhanced by passing through death's door: "And that same sociality which exists among us here will exist among us there, only it will be coupled with eternal glory, which glory we do not now enjoy" (D&C 130:2).

4. Death reminds us of the purpose of life. We know that we are mortal, but in the fast lane of life we tend to forget the temporary state of our existence here on earth until we are reminded by the death of a loved one. This sobering reminder causes us to review the meaning of life and our purpose in it. Each time death comes close to our view, we evaluate our own lives and where we are headed.

5. Death can be a test of our faith and commitment. Writing on this subject, President Harold B. Lee stated: "Death of a loved one is the most severe test that you will ever face, and if you can rise above your griefs and if you will trust in God, then you will be able to surmount any other difficulty with which you may be faced" (*New Era,* August 1971, p. 4).

6. Death makes us partakers of the grace of God. Only through his grace is death's dark hand overcome. As we are enfolded in the comforting arms of that grace, we gain a great appreciation for the greatness, glory, and love of Jesus and Heavenly Father. Without God's grace we would be left with no hope. But we are quickly reminded that Jesus Christ has given the free gift of resurrection to all. We realize that he not only has removed the barrier of temporal death but has also enabled us to overcome spiritual death through the Atonement. His grace, however, goes far beyond these two things. In the first hours following the death of a loved one, we realize that we cannot handle this challenge alone. We can, however, through Christ's healing influence, deal with the sorrow and hurt. As we accept him and believe in his great power, the promise of the scriptures and a prophet of God will be fulfilled:

> And you can have that certain knowledge that in due time
> God will wipe away all tears (see Revelation 7:17) and that "eye

hath not seen, nor ear heard, neither have entered into the heart of man, the things which God hath prepared for them that love him" (1 Corinthians 2:90). (Ezra Taft Benson, Conference Report, October 1974, p. 93.)

We have considered only a few reasons why we must die. There are many others that could be explored. Death is an important part of our Heavenly Father's plan. It is the door that allows us to leave this mortal life and enjoy the blessings of eternity.

30

The Atonement

During the summer months we spend a lot of time floating and fishing on the Snake River in Wyoming. A few years ago on a clear but somewhat chilly day, we were at the take-out boat ramp where the float trips end. It was still early in the season and we felt it was too cold to float, so we were there as spectators checking out the more adventurous souls floating the river that chilly day. As we watched the various boats come in, one of them caught our undivided attention. A young man in the boat was soaked from head to toe and apparently had fallen in the water on his trip down the river. His uncontrollable shivering tipped us off immediately that he was in trouble. Those of us with first aid experience knew that his body temperature had dropped to dangerous levels and hypothermia was setting in.

As the boat pulled up to the ramp, a man standing next to us sprinted to his car, grabbed a sleeping bag, and sprinted back to the ramp. The man threw the sleeping bag on the ramp and helped the boy remove his clothes except for his underwear. He instructed the boy to lay down on the sleeping bag, and the man took off his own outside clothing and crawled in the sleeping bag with the boy. He then wrapped his body around the boy and instructed others to wrap the sleeping bag around them until they were a snug cocoon. The moments that followed were tense and critical. We all watched and prayed that the boy's body temperature would respond favorably to the treatment.

Several minutes passed. The boy seemed to relax and his shivering became less severe. As he stabilized, others bundled him into a car and transported him to the nearest hospital to receive further treatment. The quick-thinking man with the sleeping bag literally saved the boy's life that day.

We all breathed a sigh of relief as they pulled away. But reflecting on this incident brought a lot of frightening "what if's" to our minds. What would have happened if the boy had been on the river by himself and no one had been at the dock when he arrived? What would have happened if the man had left the boy's wet clothes on? And even worse, what would have happened if the man would have had on wet clothes when he crawled in the bag and wrapped himself around the boy? The answers to these questions and many like them are obvious. The boy would have died.

Ecclesiastes 4:9–11 states:

> Two are better than one; because they have a good reward for their labour.
>
> For if they fall, the one will lift up his fellow: but woe to him that is alone when he falleth; for he hath not another to help him up.
>
> Again, if two lie together, then they have heat: but how can one be warm alone?

Physically, we can find ourselves in frightening situations when we are alone. The wonderful news is that spiritually we are never on our own unless we choose to be. Through the atonement of Jesus Christ, we can receive eternal life and salvation.

What the Atonement Is Not

1. The Savior and his atoning sacrifice are not far away. Jesus has stated: "Behold, I stand at the door, and knock: if any man hear my voice, and open the door, I will come in to him, and will sup with him, and he with me" (Revelation 3:20). He also taught: "For where two or

three are gathered together in my name, there am I in the midst of them" (Matthew 18:20). "Lift up your hearts and be glad, for I am in your midst" (D&C 29:5). The Savior and the effects of his atoning influence are always close by to lift us when we fall and give us warmth when we are cold. His elevating hand and warm touch will often be the saving influence that will pull us from eternal destruction. We must only be willing to open our lives to him and let him in.

2. Many blessings of the Atonement are not free gifts. Some fuse the Atonement and the Resurrection into one definition. Actually, the blessing of the Resurrection is just one facet of the Atonement. Only the gift of resurrection is a free gift to all. Paul explained this in his epistle to the Corinthians:

> But now is Christ risen from the dead, and become the first-fruits of them that slept.
>
> For since by man came death, by man came also the resurrection of the dead.
>
> For as in Adam all die, even so in Christ shall all be made alive. (1 Corinthians 15:20–22.)

The reuniting of our spirits and bodies after death in an immortal state is a free gift given to all who kept their first estate and chose to come to earth and receive a body. It matters not how a person lives, he will be resurrected.

However, forgiveness of our sins is a different matter. Those who are not willing to let Christ into their lives will find themselves alone. Christ's saving influence in our lives is based on the principle of agency. He will not force us to accept his atoning sacrifice but makes it available to all who are willing to call upon him and take upon themselves his name with full purpose of heart. Christ made this very clear when he said: "For behold, I God, have suffered these things for all, that they might not suffer if they would repent; but if they would not repent they must suffer even as I" (D&C 19:16–17).

3. The Atonement is not part of Satan's plan. In the great council held in our former life, Satan wanted to make us believe that he could save us all. Yet his plan was much like the boy on the dock—it was all wet. He is still peddling his false claims, but there is nothing in his plan that will save us. He would have us crawl in the sleeping bag

with wet clothes on, telling us that this will save us. Then he would add to our plight by wrapping us in his wet clothing. His plan brings the opposite of what we desire, for following him brings despair, heartbreak, and eventual spiritual death.

Several years ago, a number of prominent theologians were asked the question, What do you think of Jesus? Their replies startled many professed Christians. One asserted that a "true Christian" must reject the Resurrection. Another admitted that New Testament scholars were so divided on the question that one cannot say anything certain about the historical Jesus. Another scholar and teacher of Jesuit priests explained, "It is difficult to say in our age what the divinity of Jesus can mean. We are groping now for a way to express it—we just don't know." ("Easter 1966—A Quest for the True Jesus," *Newsweek,* April 11, 1966, p. 72.)

In a public opinion poll conducted by George Gallup, Jr., seven in ten adult American respondents said they believed in the divinity of Christ. But 90 percent of these said that Jesus is divine only in the sense that he embodies the best that is in all men (*Church News,* October 23, 1983). (*The Teachings of Ezra Taft Benson,* pp. 10–11.)

The world does not really understand the divine nature of Jesus Christ and his atonement. The scriptures leave no room for doubt as to his divinity and atoning sacrifice; indeed, their sole purpose is to testify of him and his atonement.

What the Atonement Is

1. The atonement of Jesus Christ is the only means by which we can be saved. The false gods of the world can offer temporary satisfaction, but they are powerless in resolving eternal matters. Only One has power to save. Elder Bruce R. McConkie described it this way:

There is one God and Father of us all, one eternal plan of salvation, one way back to heaven. And Jesus Christ is the name given by the Father whereby men may be saved. His is the only name given under heaven—either now or in the ages past, or in eternities yet unborn—whereby salvation comes. (See D&C 18:23; Moses 6:52.) (*Ensign,* November 1982, p. 33.)

2. The atonement of Jesus Christ is for the redemption of mankind. Because Christ is the Son of God and the Only Begotten in the flesh, he was able to make it possible for us to overcome both temporal and spiritual death. Elder Dallin H. Oaks described him as follows:

Jesus Christ is the Only Begotten Son of God the Eternal Father. He is our Creator. He is our Teacher. He is our Savior. His atonement paid for the sin of Adam and won victory over death, assuring resurrection and immortality for all men.

He is all of these, but he is more. Jesus Christ is the Savior, whose atoning sacrifice opens the door for us to be cleansed of our personal sins so that we can be readmitted to the presence of God. He is our Redeemer. (*Ensign,* November 1988, p. 65.)

As we accept Jesus Christ as our Redeemer and live to the fullest the principles that he taught, we too can become like him. The effects of the Atonement in our lives will make it possible for us to someday realize this promise found in the New Testament: "Beloved, now are we the sons of God, and it doth not yet appear what we shall be: but we know that, when he shall appear, we shall be like him" (1 John 3:2).

This promise of becoming like Jesus is a reality because of the great plan of our Father in Heaven. As discussed in previous chapters, he has established a world of opposition that allows us to grow and become strong. As we follow his commandments and participate in his ordinances, we begin to develop the attributes of Deity.

Realizing that we would sin and lack the spiritual strength to become celestial by ourselves, Jesus makes available to us the cleansing and enabling power of the Atonement. Through this great gift we may receive not only a cleansing of our sins but also a new heart and the power to become like our Father. As we strive to do the things that are discussed in this book, we should never forget that without Christ we could never gain eternal life. However, with Christ, and a consistent effort on our part, all of the Lord's promised blessings will be ours.

Works Cited

Benson, Ezra Taft. *The Gospel Teacher and His Message.* Salt Lake City: The Church of Jesus Christ of Latter-day Saints, 1976.

———. *The Teachings of Ezra Taft Benson.* Salt Lake City: Bookcraft, 1988.

Bible Dictionary, LDS edition of the King James Version of the Bible, 1979.

BYU 1988–89 Devotional and Fireside Speeches. Provo: Brigham Young University Press, 1989.

BYU 1989–90 Devotional and Fireside Speeches. Provo: Brigham Young University Press, 1990.

Church News. Salt Lake City: The Church of Jesus Christ of Latter-day Saints.

Durrant, George. *Love at Home—Starring Father.* Salt Lake City: Bookcraft, 1976.

Hartshorn, Leon R., comp. *Outstanding Stories by General Authorities.* 3 vols. Salt Lake City: Deseret Book Co., 1970–73.

History of the Church. 7 vols. Salt Lake City: The Church of Jesus Christ of Latter-day Saints.

Hymns of The Church of Jesus Christ of Latter-day Saints. Salt Lake City: The Church of Jesus Christ of Latter-day Saints, 1985.

Journal of Discourses. 26 vols. London: Latter-day Saints' Book Depot, 1854–86.

Kimball, Edward L. and Andrew E. Kimball, Jr. *Spencer W. Kimball.* Salt Lake City: Bookcraft, 1977.

Kimball, Spencer W. *The Miracle of Forgiveness.* Salt Lake City: Bookcraft, 1969.

———. *The Teachings of Spencer W. Kimball.* Edited by Edward L. Kimball. Salt Lake City: Bookcraft, 1982.

———. *We Should Be a Reverent People.* Salt Lake City: The Church of Jesus Christ of Latter-day Saints, 1976.

Lee, Harold B. *Youth and the Church.* Salt Lake City: Deseret Book Co., 1953.

McConkie, Bruce R. *Choose an Eternal Companion.* Brigham Young University Speeches of the Year. Provo: Brigham Young University Press, 1966.

———. *Common Consent.* Salt Lake City: The Church of Jesus Christ of Latter-day Saints, 1973.

———. *How to Get Personal Revelation.* Brigham Young University Speeches of the Year. Provo: Brigham Young University Press, 1966.

———. *Mormon Doctrine,* 2d ed. Salt Lake City: Bookcraft, 1966.

Rector, Hartman, Jr. *Get Up and Glow.* Brigham Young University Speeches of the Year. Provo: Brigham Young University Press, 1971.

Smith, Joseph. *Teachings of the Prophet Joseph Smith.* Selected by Joseph Fielding Smith. Salt Lake City: Deseret Book Co., 1938.

Smith, Joseph F. *Gospel Doctrine.* 5th ed. Salt Lake City: Deseret Book Co., 1938.

Smith, Joseph Fielding. *Church History and Modern Revelation.* 2 vols. Salt Lake City: The Council of the Twelve Apostles, 1953.

Stockholm Sweden Area Conference Report. Salt Lake City: The Church of Jesus Christ of Latter-day Saints, 1974.

Talmage, James E. *The Articles of Faith.* Salt Lake City: Deseret Book Co., 1958.

To Make Thee a Minister and a Witness. Melchizedek Priesthood study guide, 1990.

Young, Brigham. *Discourses of Brigham Young.* Selected by John A. Widstoe. Salt Lake City: Deseret Book, 1975.

Williams, Clyde J., comp. *The Teachings of Lorenzo Snow.* Salt Lake City: Bookcraft, 1984.

Index